THE WAY TO HEAVEN
By John Philips

COPYRIGHT INFORMATION

The Way to Heaven
By John Philips

Edited and updated by C. Matthew McMahon and Therese B. McMahon
Transcribed by Tyler Ray

Copyright © 2013 by Puritan Publications and A Puritan's Mind

Some language and grammar has been updated from the original manuscript. Any change in wording or punctuation has not changed the intent or meaning of the original author(s), and has been made to aid the modern reader.

Published by Puritan Publications
A Ministry of A Puritan's Mind
2633 Lantana Road
Crossville, TN 38572
www.apuritansmind.com
www.puritanpublications.com

All rights reserved. No part of this publication may be reproduced, stored in a retrieval system or transmitted in any form by any means, electronic, mechanical, photocopy, recording or otherwise, without the prior permission of the publisher, except as provided by USA copyright law.

This New Print Edition, 2014
Electronic Edition, 2013, 2014
Manufactured in the United States of America

ISBN: 978-1-938721-95-3
eISBN: 978-1-938721-94-6

CONTENTS

MEET JOHN PHILIPS	4
[ORIGINAL TITLE PAGE]	6
INTRODUCTORY LETTER	7
THE WAY TO HEAVEN	21
No Salvation Outside the Church	23
Election	33
Justification	35
Sanctification	40
The Means of Salvation	43
Final Remarks on the First Point	46
What the Church is	49
The Errors of the Roman Church	65
Definitions of the Church	87
True and False Doctrine	87
The Third Branch of the Definition of the Church	91
The State of the Church	93
How Men May be Added to the Church	105
The Ministry of the Word	105
Believing the Word	108
Baptism	111
The Author of This Addition to the Church	114
Be United to Christ	117

MEET JOHN PHILIPS
Edited by C. Matthew McMahon

John Philips (or Phillips) (1585-1663) was a staunch puritan during the era of the Westminster Assembly. He received his B.A. in 1603 and his M.A. in 1607 at Emmanuel College. He was first ordained as a deacon on July 16, 1609 at age 24, and then ordained as a minister on September 24, 1609. He became Rector of Wrentham, Suffolk and was at that post from 1609-1637. He was properly ejected from this living in 1662 because of nonconformity. He was, however, at that time, incapable of preaching work, because of his age and bodily infirmities, though he desired to continue in the work of the Gospel. He was chased out of England to New England for his nonconformist views, and ministered there for some years.

At his return years later to England, he brought back with him of his former station, an inclination to the New England Discipline. Overall, he was a very profitable and useful preacher. His sufferings made him study the *Ecclesiastical Points* in controversy more and more.

He married Elizabeth the sister of Dr. William Ames and by his means had no small furtherance in his studies. An intimate acquaintance with him increased his inclination to the congregational form of government after Westminster dissolved in later years as a result of the confrontation with Oliver Cromwell. He died in 1663, aged about seventy eight.

The known works of John Philips are two in number: his very famous work, 1. *The Way to Heaven*, originally published in 1625; and, 2. *The Christian's ABC's*, published in 1629.

[ORIGINAL TITLE PAGE]

THE
WAY TO
HEAVEN:

SHOWING:
1. That salvation is only in the Church
2. What the Church is
3. By what means men are added to the Church
4. The Author, or Efficient of this addition
5. The time and continuance of that work
6. The happiness of those that are added to the Church

By *John Phillips*,
Bachelor of Divinity, and
Pastor of Feversham in Kent

"This is the way, walk in it," (Isa. 30:21).

LONDON,
Printed by FELIX KINGSTON
1625.

INTRODUCTORY LETTER

To the right worshipful, the Mayor, and the Ivrats with his brethren;

And, to the community of the town and port of Feversham in Kent, J. P. wishing you a happy society with the heavenly Jerusalem here and in heaven.

Happiness is the common object of every man's desire; so that, as Seneca says, *"Viuere omnes beatè volunt;"* "There is not a man that would not be happy," (Seneca, *de vita beata*, l.i.c.i.). But there are two obstacles that hinder the attainment of this desired happiness. One is, as he says well, *"Sed ad peruidendum, uit sit, quòd beatam vitam efficiat, caligant;"* "Their light is so dim that they cannot perceive what that thing is that makes man happy." The other is, *"Si viâ lapus est;"* "If a man misses the right way," in which case, *"Ipsa velocitas maioris interualli causa fit;"* "The faster he runs, the farther he is out of the way." Therefore, this wise heathen man gives good counsel; *"Decernatur itque & quò tendamus, & qua;"* "We must look both to the end whereunto we aim, as also to the way, whereby we man attain unto it."

For the course of the world is utterly against reason, *"Pecorum ritu se qui antecedentium gregem, pergentes non qua cundum ett, sed quaitur;"* "That men endued with reason should imitate the brute and unreasonable creatures, which follow one another, though it is out of the way;" as if men should go on, not considering what way they ought to go, but what way is usually gone of others. But this is, *"non adratiorem, sed ad similitudine viuere;"* "Not according to reason, but according to example;" not like men, but like apes.

Now our guide, who is *the Way, the Truth, and the Life* (John 14:6); and therefore a better instructor than the wisest heathen has directed us Christians both to the end and to the way leading to that end, which is indeed *true happiness*, and consists in the fruition of God, by the means of saving knowledge and grace in this life, (*cf.* Psa. 144:15, John 17:3), with the rest of the Church Militant here in earth; so that if we follow his direction, we shall know, *& quò & qua*, both with and by what way we must go to attain true felicity. "Here below," as St. Augustine says, "by faith, and hereafter above, by sight," (Aug. *De Ciu. Dei.* l.19.c.27.).

And this is the scope, which I have propounded to myself in this treatise, that I might not only by lively voice say, "This is the way: walk in it;" but, as it were, by the hand, lead you in the way. For I am obliged by the bond of duty, as being your pastor, and you my flock, both to pray for you and to direct you, the best I can, in this heavenly course. Which, as I have carefully endeavored to do among you, by the space of almost twenty years; so I wish I may with good success happily continue to our mutual joys through God's blessing. For I can truly say with the apostle, "My heart's desire, and prayer to God for you, is, that ye might be saved." (Rom. 10:1); and with the prophet Samuel, "God forbid that I should sin against the Lord, and cease praying for you: but I will show you the good and right way."

Give me leave, then, I exhort you to stir up your Christian minds to an unfeigned desire and endeavor to enter into this way, tending to life and happiness. In worldly benefits we would not have others to go before us; why should we not have as great, no, greater care of heavenly things? Our savior upbraided the chief of the Jews, so that publicans and harlots went into the Kingdom of God before them (Matt. 21:31-32). "And what a shame it is," as St. Augustine says, "That simple idiots should snatch heaven from us, and we with all our knowledge and learning should be plunged into hell?" O! let us not do ourselves so great an injury. "It is the property of worldlings, who do not live according to faith," as Augustine speaks, "to angle for all their peace and property, in the sea of temporal profits, whereas the righteous live in full expectation of the glory to come." Which that you may also do, take for your furtherance this weak help in good worth; use it, and peruse it. I hope you shall find your labor well bestowed.

The occasion of this work was the burial of our neighbor, Master Edward Lapworth, Doctor of medicine; it is for the method and matter, the very same, that was then publicly delivered by lively voice, but is now not only amplified by the access of those things that the strictness of time would not then permit, but is also farther enlarged into a convenient treatise; the weight of the matter and the fitness of these times so requiring it.

If any desire to know the reason of publishing it, I must ingenuously confess, it was never liberally intended on my part, but rather extorted and pressed from me. For had it not been for a furious and over-hasty midwife that drew it out of the womb by violence, this embryo would have never seen the light. Yet when I did call to mind that Samson's lion had honey in it, so that out of the eater came forth meat, and out of the strong came forth sweetness (Judges 14:8), I willingly set on this work, hoping that by the blessing of God, some wholesome food and sweet repast might issue out of these bitter beginnings, to the refreshing of the hungry soul.

But to leave parables, and to speak plainly, this gentleman deceased was noted of all that knew him to be inclined to the Romish religion. At the funeral, I took occasion to speak something of the deceased, which either of simple misprision or sinister acceptation, was misconstrued, and by some officious hearers, carried as news to them, whose ears are patient, and gates wide open to receive the tale-bearer. On this the poor predicant was rated, as if it had been a schoolboy, by some austere pedantic; and yet the censor had nothing to object, *praeter auditum*, but only by bare hearsay. Not one auditor objected anything against the teacher; but some godly and well-minded, showing their acceptance, did give him thanks for his labors.

Now, as we see, the criminations or faults that were objected were the following:

1. That the deceased party was condemned, being accounted a papist, yes, and a seducer. The truth is, there was not so much as one word of condemnation given him, where at Momus himself might cavil (as the studious and ingenuous reader may here see by the simple truth faithfully related) unless any will be so censorious as to tax St. Paul for saying, as the truth was, that the barbarians were courteous, and showed them that had suffered shipwreck no little kindness (Acts 28:2).

That it is said that he was noted to be a papist, whoever denied it? The proposition was not that he was no papist, but (according to the doctrine of our Christian Reformed Churches) that a simple-hearted papist, not holding the whole mystery of the Romish iniquity, but only erring in some lesser points, which did not overthrow the foundation, may on repentance in general, of sins known and not known, find mercy with God, relying on Christ alone for salvation.

Where it is said that he was a seducer, I have myself charged him with it; but he was so far from maintaining that bad office that he did in excuse of himself affirm that he knew no cause why any man should count him a papist, unless it were for keeping the King's laws, in abstaining from fish on Fridays, and such like times. I call God to record, I do the man no wrong but testify in this the very truth; and expostulated with him, that if the conscience of the King's laws so prevailed with him in that, why should it not also cause him to come more often to the church, the reason being the same for both; to all this his answer was silence.

But for the matter of seducing: it does not make a man by and by a settled professor in his religion, because he labors to draw others to it. For we see by experience that if any conceive well of a religion, and begin to entertain it, though they are as yet but very novices, they will presently seek to induce others to the same. This may appear by those that were converts to the truth, as Andrew and Philip and the like (John 1:41, 45), whom as apes these erring people imitate.

2. To the former another aspersion was added, which did touch the whole ministry, and was urged with no little spite and clamor, viz., that any man, though he is never so vile, of a priestly cloth and a Roman fee shall at his funeral be commended and extolled to the heavens. If any are guilty of this crime, let him bear his own burden; for my part, I have learned with Elihu not to give titles lest my Maker should become my destroyer, for there is a woe denounced against them that speak good of evil and call darkness light (Job 32:22, Isa. 5:20).

It is well known that for diverse years I did utterly abstain from speaking any one word of the dead, but only applied myself to the instruction of the living; insomuch as it grew distasted. Yet I never did abstain, as holding unlawful. For I know there is a very good use of it: 1. that the virtues of the godly may be propounded for imitation. That we might be followers of the saints, who through faith and patience have inherited the promises. 2. That the perseverance of the faithful, being made known, we may with the ancient church, as is noted afterwards in this treatise, sing laudably to God that, being faithful to death, they have received the crown of life. 3. That if any having lived scandalously in open sin, but, through the mercy of God, by the means of his affecting rod, are recovered and brought home with the prodigal, the congregation being made acquainted with it may glorify God that has given them repentance to life and, with the angels, rejoice at the conversion of a sinner. 4. That on any extraordinary accident, men being suddenly surprised by death, their example propounded, may be a monitory to the living that they may take it to heart and profit by it. These and the same are good occasions of the teacher's discourse in this kind. And on this ground, I have endeavored to avoid *scandalum datum*, the giving of any offence, keeping myself always in the mean, or middle way, between both extremes.

3. A third crimination, or fault objected, and that with no little asperity, was that even the very profane should make a scoff of it. And what did they? Why, listen to this, being on their ale-benches, they call for another pot, deriding the doctrine of God's mercy and patience, in that he does not call everyone at once (Isa. 22:12-13), but some even at the eleventh hour. Did not the wicked do this, even at the preaching of the prophets and apostles, yes, of Christ himself (2 Pet. 3:3)? Can any pretend piety and take part with such impiety, taking it up and casting it as dung in the face of God himself? For it is not Moses, but God against whom men open their foul mouths; and the contemptuous usage of the poorest servants he counts as a sin done to himself, however men slobber it over.

4. A fourth crimination was that I should show so much respect to one that was a noted enemy to myself. But be

it that he was so; I have learned of my Master, though he were my enemy, yet to call him friend (Matt. 26:50). Could he be a greater enemy to me than Saul to David? Yet see how David gives him his due praise in his mournful song upon the death of Saul and Jonathan (2 Sam 1:23-24).

5. The next objection was that his not coming to church was excused, for that his memory was decayed. In this point I cannot tell whether I should blame more the *reporter laesum inenium*, or *laesam memoriam*, his lack of wit, or his lack of memory. For what reason is there to think that a papist should refrain from coming to church because he cannot remember what he hears? When, in truth, he would willingly be there stark deaf or learn the art of oblivion. But the truth is that the failing of his memory was spoken of in the beginning; his not coming to church, in the end of all the speech, and almost the last point, and it was applied only to his faculty, in which I said he practiced with good liking until through weakness his memory began to fail.

But the substance of the speech which I now come to will clear all. You may therefore please to understand that the sermon being ended (according to my usual manner), I took occasion to speak somewhat of the party deceased, not by way of commendation or excuse in regard of his religion, which I had before taxed for many errors, but only by way of application of one special point in my sermon, which was that in a corrupt church some may be saved, holding the foundation, though tainted with diverse errors of less moments; and so consequently in the Romish church, provided that they hold not the whole mystery of that iniquity, not by any doctrine or practice overthrow the fundamental grounds of faith and religion. This I did apply to the person of the gentleman deceased, charitably discerning him to be in the number of these, and that (as I did take it) for good reason.

    The effect of his speech concerned him was digested into these two branches: his faculty and his religion. For the first, I only touched on it in a few words, showing that he did practice the art of medicine with good and commendable acceptance, till such time as, through weakness, his memory began to fail; that he was courteous, and ready to afford his best help, especially to scholars, as I could testify of mine own certain knowledge; and not lacking in this to poor neighbors, as I had partly seen with mine own eyes, and near-dwellers to him could testify.

    Touching his religion, I did endeavor to express my charity, with our Christian Reformed Church, that all men might see the difference between Christian and Antichristian religion. They cast down headlong into hell all that do not consort with them, in dependence on one head, the Roman bishop, we charitably and hopefully conceive that in their midst, not withstanding their error of that dependence, yet many have been, are, and shall be saved, the Lord having his thousands among them that never bowed their knee to Baal.

My reasons why I did so charitably judge of his estate before God briefly these:

1. First, I showed that he was not infected with the whole mystery of iniquity, nor did appear to be obdurate and obstinate that way, because in our Christian families where he came, he was known to join with them in prayer.

2. In conference and dispute about religion, every man that did converse with him can testify his unskillfulness and weakness that way; in which his disabilities of answer were usually supplied, with these or such like evading speeches: "God send us all to heaven," "The Son of God be good to us," etc.

3. He protested to me that he was never at the most solemn part of their Romish religion, that is, the Mass; nor did he ever know what it meant. This confession was not long before his death.

4. His skill in the utensils and vessels of their religious service was so little that he did not know a chalice, but would pleasantly tell of his mistake, taxed by a gentlewoman, better skilled in the trade than himself.

5. Myself reading to him a sermon of St. Bernard, in which the father vehemently inveighed against the court and

prelacy of Rome, and demanding of him whether Luther, or Calvin, or any of our men could more plainly and more powerfully speak against such impiety, he did as a man convicted, admire it as strange to him; for he saw there was no deceit, inasmuch as it was read to him in his own book.

6. He ordinarily (though not so often as was fit) resorted to church, and communicated annually, excepting the last year or little more before his death; and that was on occasion of the prince's going into Spain, which made many befool themselves.

7. Last of all, in the shutting up of his life, near his end, myself praying with him, he did show his consent by erecting both his hands up to heaven, and after the prayer ended by giving me his hand cheerfully and willingly of his own accord.

If these are not sufficient arguments to induce my charity towards him, judge you. And tell me, I pray you, whether such a speech, so charitably uttered, need to flee the light and be of the cover of darkness; or rather with boldness come into the light, as it now does, that it may be approved of God and discreet good men.

That I may not with too much prolixity offend your patience, I will now draw to an end, entreating your courteous acceptance of this token of my sincere love to you. It is indeed in many ways due unto you of right, but especially in regard of your love and kind respect shown to me of late;

that, whereas for the space of above ten years, I constantly continued the weekly lecture upon the market day, having no recompense for that pains but only Master William Sakers' legacy of five pounds per annum, it hath pleased you, upon due consideration, to augment it to a convenient stipend: which good work was first well begun by Master Reginold Edwards, and that not only mentioned by word, but seconded by his liberal act, in contributing most largely to so good a purpose. And whereas voluntary contributions, depending only upon the donor's free disposition, are in like manner as charity itself, subject to wax cold; it was not only very kindly towards me, but exceeding providently for the better continuance of so religious a work, propounded by Master William Thurston to the whole corporation, and by their general consents condescended to it, that the stipend should ever hereafter be paid out of the chamber. Of which pious work, I commend to the world this monument in the just praise both of those prime motors, as also of you all, who were the concomitants and helpful causes of that so good and needful a furtherance of God's religious service; desiring the Almighty to bless you all, and to give you the comfort that religious Nehemiah had in the like case—that with him, every one of you may be able to say unto God with joy and confidence, " Remember me, O my God, concerning this, and wipe not out my good deeds that I have done for the house of my God, and for the offices thereof," (Neh. 13:14).

Yours in the Lord Jesus,

John Phillips

THE WAY TO HEAVEN

Acts 2:47, "And the Lord added to the Church daily such as should be saved."

There is nothing more fit, nor better beseeming a Christian mind at such times and on such occasions as this, when our mortality is set before our eyes, than to consider seriously with ourselves what shall become of us after this life. That seeing our passage out of this world by death is inevitable, we may, before our departure, learn here on earth how to live forever in heaven.

This heavenly lesson is taught here in this short and sweet text, that I may open to you, and in opening it, may set open heaven's gate to every faithful one; you shall understand that these words are the conclusion of a memorable history concerning the prime and first gathering together of the Christian Church by the Apostles, after the glorious ascension of our Lord and Savior Jesus Christ.

Know therefore that to the end that so great a work as the converting of the whole world, consisting of many nations and different languages, might be better effected, our blessed Lord did, according to his promise, send the Holy Spirit on the Apostles, enabling them to speak to every nation (Luke 24:49, Acts 1:4-5) and people in their own tongues, that all countries might be taught to know and worship God in their own language (Acts 2:4, 11). And for the greater encouragement of the Apostles, it pleased God to give such a blessing to these beginnings that about *three thousand* souls were converted at the first sermon of Peter (Acts 2:41).

Now, to show that this blessing did not cease there, but that it continued still, and shall continue to the end of the world, it is said in the shutting up of this history that "the Lord added to the Church daily such as should be saved."

These words offer unto us at the first view four remarkable *observations:*

The first is the way to salvation; and that is, by being added to the Church.

The second is the Efficient Author of this addition, and that is *the Lord God.*

The third is the time and continuance of this work; and that is καθ' ἡμέραν, daily, or from day to day.

The fourth is the happy end of such as are added to the Church, and that is *salvation.* They all, and they *only*, are such as shall be saved.

NO SALVATION OUTSIDE THE CHURCH

In the first observation, that I may complete the whole doctrine of it, three things are to be considered. 1. That the way to salvation is by the Church. 2. What that Church is where salvation may be had. 3. By what means and how men are to be added to the Church that they may be saved.

Touching the first branch, it must be known and believed of all that desire salvation that the *Regia via*, the King of kings' *highway to heaven* is the Church, without which Church, *there is no salvation.*

That I may demonstrate this truth, cast but your eye on the ark of Noah, in which was most lively figured the Church of God. A type, twice alleged by Saint Peter, to this very purpose: *to show that salvation is and only is in the Church.* And therefore he urges against such as made defection from the Church that God did not spare the old world, but brought in the flood on the world of the ungodly, that is, on those who were out of the ark—out of the Church (2 Pet. 2:5, Gen. 7:23).

Again, baptism, being the sacrament of our entrance into the Church of Christ, he parallels it and compares it with the ark, intimating this much, that as only those eight souls were saved in the ark by water, so there is no hope of salvation but only in the Church (1 Pet. 3:20-21); the solemn entrance into which is ordinarily by baptism (Eph. 2:12, 4:5).

We know that the head is the fountain of life, sense, and motion to the whole body and every member of it, but yet only to that body of which it is the head. Even so it is between Christ and the Church; Christ is the head, the Church is the body, and every true Christian is a particular member of that body (Col. 1:18, Eph. 1:22-23). "Ye are," St. Paul says, "the body of Christ, and members in particular," (1 Cor. 12:27). Now, as the head does naturally perform the office of a head to the body, and to it only, so Christ imparts the divine influence of saving grace only to his Church. Therefore, the Apostle, speaking of Christ, says, "That from the head, all the body by joints and bands, having nourishment ministered and knit together, increaseth with the increase of God," (Eph. 4:16); and having affirmed that "Christ is the head of the Church," (Eph. 5:23), he immediately infers on it, and he is "the Savior of the body." "This is that body, out of which the spirit giveth no life" (Gregory in Psa. 5, *paen.* "*Iflud est corpus, extra quod non vivificat spiritus.*").

This position, that salvation is to be had only in the Church, is not obscurely noted by those sacred families, so frequent in scripture, where the Church is resembled to a house; to a city, to a mother, to a vine.

To a house: so St. Paul calls it the *house of God*, which is the Church of the living God (1 Tim. 3:15).

It is likened to a house in a twofold sense: first, as the word is taken properly for an edifice or mansion, and building to dwell in, consisting of foundation, walls, and roof; so St. Peter terms it the faithful "lively stones built up a spiritual house; and Christ, the corner stone," (1 Pet. 2:5-6). Paul calls them "God's building;" himself and other ministers, "God's builders;" and Christ, "the foundation:" for, he says, "other foundations can no man lay, than that is laid, which is Jesus Christ," (1 Cor. 3:9-11); and he tells the Ephesians that they are "built upon the foundation of the Apostles and prophets, Christ himself being the chief corner stone," (Eph. 2:20).

As therefore the safety of a house stands in the strength and firmness of its own foundation, which gives support to it, and only to it; even so salvation and freedom from eternal and utter ruin belongs only to the Church, the House of God, built firmly on the rock Jesus Christ, that "the gates of hell cannot prevail against it," (Matt. 16:18).

Again, it is compared to a house in another sense; the word "house" being taken for the inhabitants; so it is understood when Peter says that "judgment must begin in the house of God;" that is, with the godly—with the *righteous*—as he plainly interprets himself (1 Pet. 4:17). And the Apostle to the Hebrews, calling the Church Christ's "own house," says of himself and the rest of the faithful, "whose house we are." Now, the Church and every member of it is called *the house of God*, and of Christ, because he dwells in their hearts by faith, as a householder in his house (Eph. 3:17). More expressly elsewhere in plain terms, the Church is called "the Lord's family," or "household" (Matt. 24:45), "the domestics," or "household of God" (Eph. 2:19), "the household of faith" (Gal. 6:10); the ministers are called "stewards that rule over the household;" and Christ himself "the Lord of the house" (Luke 12:43).

As, then, the master of a family provides only for his own house, all necessities for maintenance and sustenation of life; but not for others, or other men's families, except it is in the case of charity. So God, though in his gracious indulgence, as a Creator to his creatures, he is "good to all," (Psa. 145:9); he "preserveth man and beast," (Psa. 36:6): he "maketh his sun to rise on the evil and on the good, and sendeth rain on the just and on the unjust," (Matt. 5:45). Yet in a peculiar manner he "is good to Israel, even to such as are of a clean heart," (Psa. 73:1). He "is the savior of all men, but especially of those that believe," (1 Tim. 4:10). Only this household of faith he saves eternally; they only, having God for their Father, the Church for their Mother, Christ for their elder Brother, regenerated by one and the same immortal seed of the Word of God, nourished with one and the same sincere milk, partakers all of one bread, and drinking one cup. Therefore, Peter says of himself, and the rest of this family that God "according to his divine power, hath given unto us all things that pertain unto life and godliness, through the knowledge of him that hath called us to glory and virtue." None, then, can look for life and salvation, but they that are of God's household, who alone can truly say with the Psalmist, "I am thine, save me," (Psa. 119:94).

The Church is likewise resembled to a city or commonwealth; so it is set forth in a vision to Saint John, by the name of the holy city, New Jerusalem; that great city, the holy Jerusalem (Rev. 21:2, 10); So again it is called the City of the Living God, the Heavenly Jerusalem (Heb. 12:22).

It is compared to a city in two respects; that is to say, defense and privilege.

We know that cities are places of refuge (Num. 32:17), to defend the inhabitants from the force of enemies (Jer. 4:5, 8:14). So is the Church to the true members of it the only place of eternal safety. Therefore, it is that the faithful in their triumphant song do to the praise of God sing in this manner: "We have a strong city, salvation will God appoint for walls and bulwarks," (Isa. 26:1). And the prophet Joel, foretelling the state of the Christian Church says, "In Mount Sion and in Jerusalem shall be deliverance," (Joel 2:32). So that in this heavenly city, entered into here on earth, is our only security of salvation; without it, there can be no safety at all. On this Saint Augustine, alluding to the words of the Psalm which says, "Praise the Lord, O Jerusalem; praise thy God, O Sion: for he hath made fast the bars of thy gates," (Psa. 147:12-13). "When," he says, "the bars of the gates are fast, as none can come in, so none can go out" (Aug. *de Ciu. Dei*, l.19.c.11.); intimating by this that they that do not belong to this City of God, the Church, but remain without, cannot have the benefit of defense, but lie open to all eternal ruin; where, on the contrary, they that are so in it, that are also of it, can never be surprised by an enemy, but many sing comfortably with David, "Blessed be the Lord, for he hath shown me his marvelous kindness, in a strong," or fenced, "city," (Psa. 31:21).

Again, cities or commonwealths have their privileges, immunities, and freedoms, wherein the citizens and freemen only are interested. To this purpose, that Father citeth the definition of *Scipio* in *Tullie de Rep. Respublica, est res populi.* That is, "The wealth-public is the people's wealth." Or thus: "The commonwealth is the wealth or welfare of the commons." It is so with the Church. Therefore, of this immunity and freedom, the Apostle, speaking of the catholic Church says, "Jerusalem which is above is free" (Gal. 4:26); and telling the Ephesians that before their conversion, they "were without Christ, and were aliens from the commonwealth of Israel, and were strangers from the covenant of promise, and had no hope, and were without God in the world," he says, "but now in Christ Jesus, ye which were far off are made near by the blood of Christ," and afterward adds these words: "Now therefore ye are no more strangers and foreigners, but citizens with the saints;" meaning by it that they had now, being entered into the Church, attained to the immunity and freedom of the City of God (Eph. 2:12-13, 19). But where in this consists this freedom? Among other privileges, it mainly and principally consists in freedom from sin and condemnation for sin; it is here that Paul assures the faithful that sin shall have no dominion over them, and that being freed from sin, they have their fruit in holiness, and the end everlasting life (Rom. 6:14, 22). Again, that there is "no condemnation to them that are in Christ Jesus," (Rom. 8:1). By this it is evident that the privilege of eternal life and happiness is the peculiar right of the City of God, the Church.

It is also likened to a mother. So the Apostle says, "that Jerusalem which is above, is the mother of us all," (Gal. 4:26). This resemblance stands in two things.

First, the Church, as a mother, conceives and brings forth children to God by the immortal seed of the Word of God, in the ministry of the Church (1 Pet. 1:23); whereunto St. Paul alluding, says to the Galatians, "My little children, of whom I travail in birth again, until Christ be formed in you," (Gal. 4:19).

Secondly, the Church, as a mother after her children are borne and brought forth, feeds and nourishes them with the sincere milk of the Word of God out of her two breasts, the Sacred Scriptures of the Old and New Testament (*cf.* 1 Pet. 2:2; Augustine *in Esp. Joh. Tract 3. Est water Ecclesia, & verba eius, duo testamenta divinarum Scripturarums*); and as they grow in strength, give them not only milk, but also strong meat (Heb. 5:12, 14).

As therefore no man can live the life of nature, but he must have a mother, by whom he must be conceived and brought forth into the world, and must with it have convenient nourishment for preservation of life, so no man can live the life of grace here and the life of glory forever, unless he is borne of his mother, the Church, and nourished in it, to everlasting life. To this purpose is that noted saying of an ancient Father, "He shall never have God for his Father that hath not the Church for his mother."

The Church is again compared to a vine, as we may see by the complaint of the faithful to God in the Psalm, "Thou hast brought a vine out of Egypt...why hast thou then broke down her hedges?" (Psa. 80:8, 12). And God's complaint concerning his Church, "O inhabitants of Jerusalem, and men of Judah, judge, I pray you, between me and my vineyard: when I looked that it should bring forth grapes, it brought forth wild grapes," (Isa. 5:3-4). Our Savior Christ, under the parable of the vine, describes the Church, likening himself to the body or stalk, and the members of his Church to the branches. "I am," he says, "the vine and ye are the branches," (John 15:5). This is inferred on the words going before, noting the due proportion between the vine and the Church. "As the branch," says Christ, "cannot bear fruit of itself except it abide in the vine; no more can ye, except ye abide in me," (verse 4). This he further amplifies in these words, "He that abideth in me, and I in him, the same bringeth forth much fruit; for without me ye can do nothing. If a man abide not in me, he is cast forth as a branch, and is withered, and men gather them and cast them into the fire, and they are burned," (verses 5-6). All this imports this much, that unless we are engrafted into Christ, the true vine, and so become lively branches in the body of the Church, we can have no hope of life and salvation, "for," says St. Augustine, "outside of this body, the Holy Spirit quickens no man," (*Aug. Ep. 50. ad. Boniface*).

This doctrine of salvation in the Church only is not only thus illustrated by the bright-shining light of so many divine similitudes and parables, but is also warranted by evident and invincible reason, grounded on the word of God.

1. It is a principle undeniable *that there is only one saving truth*. And therefore the Apostle says that all men whom God will have saved, he will have "to come to the knowledge of the truth," (1 Tim. 2:4). Now this truth is nowhere to be found but

in the Church of God. It is here that the godly are termed "the righteous nation, that keepeth the truth," (Isa. 16:2). And Paul describes the Church "the pillar and ground of truth," (1 Tim. 3:15). And for this cause, the Spirit by which the Church is guided is called "the Spirit of truth;" and it was promised by our Lord Christ that it should come and guide the Church "into all truth," (John 16:13). If then there can be no salvation without the knowledge of the truth, and no saving truth but only in the Church, it consequently follows that there is no salvation out of the Church.

2. There are certain graces that accompany salvation (Heb. 6:9) which are the peculiar of the Church of God; they may be all included in these four, that is. The grace of *election*, the grace of *vocation*, the grace of *justification*, and the grace of *sanctification*; all of which jointly and independently have their period and end in *glorification*.

This we may plainly see by that golden chain of man's salvation in the Epistle to the Romans, of which not one link can be broken by the greatest power of hell, "Whom God did predestinate," the Apostle says, "them he also called; and whom he called, them he also justified; ad whom he justified, them he also glorified," (Rom. 8:30).

That these graces are concomitant to salvation, and the peculiar of the Church, is not only manifest for the general, by this golden chain, never worn of any but the faithful; but it will more evidently appear if we examine the particulars.

ELECTION

As for *predestination* and *election*, by which God chooses men to salvation of his free grace and mercy, without any merit in man; it is so proper to the Church, that Peter calls it "a chosen generation, a peculiar people," (1 Pet. 2:9). Paul says of the Church that they are "chosen of God in Christ, before the foundation of the world; according to the good pleasure of his will; to the praise of the glory of his grace," (Eph. 1:4). Our Savior, distinguishing the sound members of the Church from the hypocrites, such as Judas, says, "I speak not of you all; I know whom I have chosen," (John 13:18): and of the faithful, he says, "Ye have not chosen me, but I have chosen you, and ordained you," (John 15:16).

Then to be a sound member of the Church and to be elect is all one; and not to be elect, though in the Church, is no benefit to salvation. Therefore St. Luke, having said in our text that "the Lord added to the Church such as should be saved," says afterward in equivalent phrase of speech that "as many as were ordained to eternal life believed," (Acts 13:48). To this accords that saying of St. Gregory, speaking of the church,

"Within the limits," he says, "are all the elect, without them are all the reprobate; yea, although they may seem to be within the bounds of faith," (Greg. Mor. I. 28. c. 6. *Intra has mensuras, sunt omness elcti, extra has sunt omnes reprobi, eliamsintra fiaei limiten esse vdeantur*). It is no marvel, then, though St. Peter, advising the faithful to secure their own salvation, counsels them to do it by giving diligence to make their calling and election sure (2 Pet. 1:10).

Touching *vocation,* or *calling,* I mean effectual calling, the effect of election, by which God converts the souls of men to himself, calling them out of the society of the world, into the communion of the saints, as it were, out of the darkness into light (1 Pet. 2:9); it is also such a property of the Church that it cannot possibly be separated from it. Therefore, the Church is said to be "the called of Jesus Christ," (Rom. 1:6), and to be those who are "called according to the purpose" of God (Rom. 8:28), and "partakers of the heavenly vocation," (Heb. 3:1).

Now, that it is a companion of salvation is evident by that exhortation of the Apostle, exciting the faithful that they "would walk worthy of God, who hath called *them* unto his kingdom and glory," where we may see that glorification is the *terminus ad quem*, that is, the end to which tends the calling of God's people. And that they shall never fail of this end, he secures them by the fidelity of the caller, "God," he says, "is faithful, by whom ye were called unto the fellowship of his son Jesus Christ our Lord," (1 Cor. 1:9). And again, "faithful is he that calleth you, who also will do it," (1 Thess. 5:24). And therefore the Apostle, speaking of graces that accompany salvation, and by name of *effectual vocation*, the fruit of election, confidently assures the Romans that "the gifts and calling of God are without repentance," (Rom. 11:29). A text so clear for the inseparability of God's effectual calling and consequent salvation, that our *Rhenish* adversaries, who everywhere catch anything that may but seem to make for themselves, or against us, are here, upon this verse, constrained to be mute, and say nothing, but only leave a blank (*cf.* Rhen. on Rom. 11:29).

JUSTIFICATION

We come now to *justification*. It is a word of great variety for its signification, but we need not trouble ourselves with no more but this one distinction. It is either that by which we stand just before God, or that whereby we are declared to be just before men. The former is properly justification; the latter is called sanctification. Yet both are *sometimes* included under the name justification, as we may see by that golden chain of the Apostle, before cited, "Whom he called, them he also justified; and whom he justified, them he also glorified," (Rom. 8:30); otherwise the chain had been imperfect, and had lacked a main link, without which, glorification could not follow. This distinction of justification before God and before men is grounded on the words of St. Paul, "If Abraham were justified by works, he hath whereof to glory, but not before God," (Rom. 4:2); and it fitly reconciles St. Paul and St. James, the one speaking of justification before God, which we have now in hand; the other, of justification before men, or sanctification, which we shall touch in the next place.

Now concerning justification before God, we are to consider both what it is that it is proper to the Church, as also that it is a necessary antecedent of salvation.

Justification, then, is an action of God, by which he, pardoning all sins, imputes righteousness to every true believer, out of his free grace and mercy, only on the merit of Jesus Christ.

The branches, being many, require distinct explication.

1. It is an action of God. It intimates the Apostle, "Who," he says, "shall lay anything to the charge of God's elect? It is God that justifieth," (Rom. 8:33).

2. It consists in the pardon of sins. To this purpose the same Apostle alleges the Psalm. "As David," he says, "declareth

the blessedness of the man, to whom God imputeth righteousness without works;" saying, "Blessed are they whose iniquities are forgiven, and whose sins are covered. Blessed is the man to whom the Lord will not impute sin."

3. It is a mere imputation of righteousness, outside of man, in Christ Jesus alone, that causes a man to stand just in the sight of God, and not any merit of works in man himself; for, as was said before, to constitute a blessed man, God imputes righteousness without works (Rom. 4:6). This imputed righteousness, not inherent in us, but out of us, in Christ, is expressly noted by St. Paul, where he says that Christ "who knew no sin, was made sin for us, that we might be made the righteousness of God in him," (2 Cor. 5:21). Make a note of two things here, says St. Augustine, "The righteousness of God, not our righteousness: in him, not in us." So then, look how Christ was made sin for us, in the same manner are we made the righteousness of God in him; but Christ was not made sin by infusion or inherency of sin, but only by imputation. So we, that we may be saved, must be justified, not by our inherent righteousness, which at the best is imperfect; but by the imputed righteousness of Christ "who of God is made unto us wisdom, righteousness, sanctification, and redemption," (1 Cor. 1:30).

4. This righteousness is imputed to every true believer: for it is faith only by which we apprehend Christ with all his

benefits, as we may see if we compare together *faith*, *hope*, and *charity*. *Faith*, like a hand, receives and lays hold on the object, Christ; therefore St. John makes receiving of Christ and believing in him all one (John 1:12). *Hope* only expects and looks for the accomplishment of that which faith believes, and with "patience waiteth for it," (Rom. 8:25). *Charity* distributes her good things to the benefit of others. It is here that faith only is said to justify, because it is the only instrumental cause of our justification, in that it alone apprehends Christ, by whom we are justified. Scriptures for this are plentiful, "from all things," says St. Paul in his sermon at Antioch, "from which ye could not be justified by the Law of Moses, by Christ, everyone that believeth, is justified," (Acts 13:39). And disputing the question of justification, he so determines it, "Therefore we conclude, that a man is justified by faith, without the deeds of the Law," (Rom. 3:28). "This," says St. Bernard, "is the Apostle's meaning: that a man is justified freely by faith," (Bern. *Serm. I. de annun. Sie Enim arbitratur Apologus gratis instifi ani hominem perfidem.*).

    5. Our justification is of God's free grace and mercy: this the Apostle anounces, that all men "are justified freely by his grace." A truth so evident that it has obtained the adversaries' ingenuous confession, "for the uncertainty of our own righteousness," says Bellarmine, "and the peril of

vainglory, it is most safe to repose our whole confidence in the sole mercy and favor of God," (*Bell. De just. 1.5.c.7. Propter incertitudine propre justitie, & periculum inanis glorie, tatiscimie est, fidu sam sotam, in sola Dei mistericordia & binignitate reponere*). So, even our adversaries being witnesses, our Christian *Reformed* Religion directs men the *safest* way to heaven.

6. It is for the only merit of Jesus Christ: therefore the Apostle having said that we are "justified by his free grace," adds, "through the redemption that is in Jesus Christ." And venerable Bede says that "Christ's death is our life, his condemnation, our justification," (Bede in *Psa.* 87 *Christi mors, nostra viva est, cius damnation, nostra justifacatio*).

So we see what justification is, now that it belongs only to the Church, and is a concomitant to salvation, our *Creed* may teach us, where we are directed to believe, as special privileges of the Catholic Church, "the forgiveness of sins, and the resurrection to life everlasting." And the Apostle says that "we being justified by his grace, should be made heirs according to the hope of eternal life," (Titus 3:7). Where we have in one text both the persons to whom justification does belong, "we," says the Apostle, that is, the Church, and faithful people of God; and the inheritance of eternal life following.

SANCTIFICATION

The last grace accompanying salvation is sanctification. It is a grace of God whereby a man, being justified, is in every part of soul and body renewed by the Spirit of God, no more to live in sin, but to walk in newness of life (1 Thess. 5:23; Rom. 6:2, 4). It is in a word, the renewed image of God, consisting in knowledge, righteousness, and true holiness (Col. 3:10; Eph. 4:24). You may see in the lesson that grace teaches all her children, which is, to deny ungodliness and worldly lusts, and to live soberly, righteously, and godly in this present world, being zealous of good works (Titus 2:11-12). Justification and sanctification differ in four points. 1. Justification is before sanctification in nature, though both be together in time; for as the branch must first be in the vine, before it can by virtue of the sap bring forth fruit: so a man must first be in Christ, by faith, before he can be a new creature, and so bring forth the fruit of holiness (John 15:4). 2. Justification is without us, in Christ, as was said before, but sanctification is within us, inherent, and infused by the Spirit of God. 3. Justification is that by which we stand absolved, and made just in the sight of God, but by sanctification we are only declared to be just. 4. Justification quiets the conscience by reconciling it, and making it at peace with God, for, "being justified by faith, we have peace towards

God through our Lord Jesus Christ." But sanctification cannot do so, because our best actions are imperfect, and in regard of their defect stand in need of pardon. "If thou, Lord, shouldest mark iniquities, O Lord, who shall stand?" (Psa. 130:3).

Now, that *sanctification* is also peculiar to the Church, hear the Apostle, showing the difference between men out of the church and such as are in it: speaking of their profaneness before their calling, he says, "and such were some of you," but telling them of their change, he adds, "but ye are washed, but ye are sanctified," (1 Cor. 6:11). It is therefore the style or addition of the Church. "Unto the Church of God," Paul says, "which is at Corinth, to them that are sanctified in Christ Jesus, called to be saints," (1 Cor. 1:1-2). And we believe in our Creed, "the holy Catholic Church, the Communion of Saints." That it accompanies salvation, is more than manifest, for without it, "no man shall see the Lord," (Heb. 12:14), but "being freed from sin, we have our fruit in holiness, and the end, everlasting life," (Rom. 6:22). Therefore, we must know that sanctification is such a necessary antecedent, though no meritorious cause, of salvation, that notwithstanding no man shall be saved without it: because true saving faith, the instrumental cause of our justification and salvation, works by love (Gal. 5:6), and can be no more without sanctity and good works than fire can be without heat, or water without moisture.

To conclude then, if there is no salvation without *election, calling, justification,* and *sanctification*; and none of these to be found, but *only in the Church of God*, it follows necessarily that there is no salvation out of the Church.

There are certain means appointed of God to work and increase saving grace, which if they shall be found to be the prerogative of the Church, it cannot be denied, but that only there salvation is to be had; for in reason, the end cannot ordinarily be attained without the means leading unto it. Our Savior, telling the woman of Samaria of the water of life, she answered him, "Sir you have nothing to draw withal, and the well is deep, from where then have you that water of life?" (John 4:11). Indeed the well is profound and deep from where we must fetch the ever-living water, and the woman's reason may teach us that we had need of instruments and means to convey it to us.

THE MEANS OF SALVATION

Now the *means* to effect and perfect man's salvation are *the written Word of God*, called *the Scriptures, the ministry of preaching the Word, the two sacraments of the New Testament,* and *prayer*. That these are means, see first for *the Word written*, what St. Paul says to the Romans, "Whatsoever things were written aforetime, were written for our learning, that we through patience and comfort of the Scriptures might have hope," (Rom. 15:4). To this purpose is that commendation of Timothy propounded for the imitation of all the faithful, that from a child he had known the Holy Scriptures which are able to make him wise to salvation (2 Tim. 3:15). Therefore, our Savior advises to "search the scriptures: for in them," he says, "ye think to have eternal life, and they are they which testify of me," (John 5:39). Touching *the ministry of preaching*, it is called by the Apostle, "the power of God unto salvation, to everyone that believeth," (Rom. 1:16; *see also* 1 Cor. 1:18). The *sacraments* are the seals of the righteousness of faith (Rom. 4:11); and so consequently of salvation. *Prayer* is that to which the promise is made, "Whosoever shall call upon the name of the Lord, shall be saved," (Rom. 10:13).

That these are the prerogatives of the Church is out of the question. "For to them are committed the oracles of God,"

(Rom. 3:2), and "he sheweth his word unto Jacob," says the Psalm, "his statutes and his judgments unto Israel. He hath not dealt so with any nation," (Psa. 147:19-20).

As for *the ministry of preaching*, God has committed it to the Apostles, and the succeeding pastors of the Church. "God", the Apostle says, "hath given unto us the ministry of reconciliation... and hath committed unto us the Word of reconciliation," (2 Cor. 5:18-19). Again, that he has set or *ordained* them in the Church and *not* elsewhere (1 Cor. 12:28), and that for the gathering together and edifying of the saints, to continue to the end of the world (Eph. 4:12-13).

That the *sacraments* are the Church's proper right is manifest: for to whom do the seals belong, but only to them that are within the covenant, of which the seals are the effectual signs and pledges? And of whom is it said, "Go and baptize them," but of those, which join themselves to the Church by believing (Matt. 28:19, Acts 2:41)? Or to whom was it ever spoken, but only to the Church, "do this in remembrance of me: eat ye, drink ye all of this, *etc*.," (Matt. 26:26-27).

Touching *prayer*, only those can pray that have true saving faith, "for how shall they call upon him," says the Apostle, "in whom they believe not," (Rom. 10:14;). And none can invocate God aright, that cannot truly and with confidence call God "Father," which none can do but they that are led by the Spirit of God, which St. Pall calls, "the Spirit of adoption, whereby we cry Abba, Father," (Rom. 8:1-15; Chemnic. *Exam. Pars. 3. p. 179. b.*) This, therefore, is the prerogative of the Church (Acts 9:14,21; Rom. 10:12), by which they are in Scripture, as by a proper note distinguished from all others. They are distinguished from both the profane, those that do not pray at all (Psa. 14:4); hypocrites, that babble with their lips, but their hearts are far from God (Matt. 6:7, 15:8); and superstitions, that invocate creatures, with confidence to be heard of them (Matt. 4:10). So the Apostle, describing the Church, among other notes, sets it forth by this, that they are such as in every place "call upon the name of Jesus Christ our Lord," (1 Cor. 1:2); and again, that "call upon the Lord, out of a pure heart," (2 Tim. 2:22). Now then, if the invocation of God, and of him alone, and that in truth, is not an essential property of the Church, and as the logicians call it, *proprium quartomodo*, proper to all and every member of it, to them alone and at all times, how can it distinguish them, as the Scripture does, from all others? (Psa. 145:18). Then we see that the means of salvation being only in the Church, salvation itself is only there, and not to be found elsewhere.

FINAL REMARKS ON THE FIRST POINT

1. To shut up this doctrine in a short sum, it must be granted by all that none can be saved that do not have Christ for their *Mediator* and *Advocate* (1 John 2:1-2); for there is none other, as there is none other but one God. So the Apostle says, "There is one God, and one mediator between God and man, the man Christ Jesus," (1 Tim. 2:5). And that he is the only Mediator of the Church, we may take it as his own word, "I pray for them, I pray not for the world: but for them which thou hast given me: for they are thine," (John 17:9). And St. Paul, speaking of himself and the rest of the faithful says that Christ is at the right hand of God, and makes intercession for us (Rom. 8:34). So by a cloud of witnesses is this divine truth confirmed, *that out of the Church, there is no salvation.*

1. Gross, therefore, and absurd is that libertine opinion that any may be saved in *any* religion, leading an outward civil life; the Turk in his Mahometism, the Jew in his Judaism, the heathen in his Paganism. They may as well say that in the *deluge* a man might have been preserved out of the ark, on some tree or house top; or that a limb separated from the body, or a branch cut off from the vine may live.

2. This also discovers the fearful and damnable estate of those who, never regarding church or religion, content

themselves as mere naturals and worldlings to enjoy the world. These *Esauites* had rather with their father Esau, please their palate with a little meat than enjoy the heavenly blessing (Heb. 12:16). They gaze on the ark with the old world; they wonder to see such pacing into it—no, as St. Augustine speaks, "They murmur and eat their galls, to see the people flock unto the Church, to those pure solemnities of Christ: where both sexes are so honestly distinguished by their several places: where they may learn how well to lead their temporal lives here, that they may become worthy of the eternal hereafter," (Augustine, *de Civit. Dei.* 2. 6. 23.). These profane ones have their eyes so blinded by the god of this world that they cannot see any other heaven but the world (2 Cor. 4:4).

3. A caveat is given here to all schismatic spirits, who for external things, as masters of order and ceremony merely adiaphorous or indifferent, separate themselves from the society of the Church. They are like some foolish and furious navigator, who in his voyage, on every occasion of discontent, casts himself overboard, presuming to be safe enough out of the ship. Let such know that though God in his mercy may save the simply seduced, as being of his invisible catholic Church, yet the roadway is to be joined with some visible orthodox congregation.

4. This calls all men with a most forcible invitation, even as ever they desire to be saved, to enter timely into this straight gate that leads to life (Matt. 7:14). Many of the Egyptians and other strangers, when they saw the great works God did for his Church, and in what safe and happy condition the people were in, they were over; they left their own country alliance and friends, and joined themselves to the Jews (Exod. 12:38). This we should do—forsake all, and follow Christ (Mark 10:28); leave all societies for the communion of the saints; for the dove found no rest for the sole of her foot, but was fain to return into the ark again (Gen 8:9): so let a man compass the whole world, yet shall he never be able to find rest to his soul, until by entering into the Church, he take Christ's yoke on him (Matt. 11:29). Let him with Solomon try all things under the sun: pleasures, riches, honors, and what the world can afford—he shall at the last be driven to cry out, "Vanity of vanities," and conclude when all is done, "Hear the end of all, fear God, and keep his commandments, for this is all of man, all his duty, and all his dignity; and without this, all that a man is, or hath, is but mere vanity," (Eccl 1:2; 12:13; Junius *in Eccl. 12. Sine quo totus homonibil est nisi vanitas.*). So much for the first branch.

WHAT THE CHURCH IS

The next branch to be considered is *what the Church is, where salvation is to be had*. A very necessary question for these times in which we live, in regard there is not a sect or faction in all the Christian world that does not challenge the name of the Church to itself.

But we must know that there is nothing more childish than to boast of the name of a thing when the thing itself is lacking. We have a maxim in logic—*A nomie ad rem non valet consequentia*. "To argue from the name to prove the thing is so, because it is so named, is an argument inconsequent." Our Savior tells the Church of Smyrna they that are there that "say they are Jews and are not, but are the Synagogue of Satan," (Rev. 2:9). And to the Church of Sardis he says, "I know thy works: for thou hast a name that thou art alive, but thou art dead," (Rev. 3:1). The Church of the Laodiceans was of all the rest of the seven Churches in the worst condition (being neither cold nor hot), as we may see in that our Savior does not give them any one commendation at all, as he does to the rest of the Churches, giving them their due praise, notwithstanding this end, both to show his detestation of lukewarmness, and that where there is lukewarmness in religion, there is no goodness to be expected. Yet the

Laodiceans, as far as they were from the true zeal of religion, notwithstanding, boasted themselves to be rich, and lacked nothing; where indeed they were *wretched, and miserable, and poor, and blind, and naked* (Rev. 3:15-17). It is therefore a very silly and simple part to take men at their bare word, as our seduced Romanists do, in so weighty a matter as religion is. The men of Berea are commended, for that they "searched the Scriptures daily, whether those things were so," or not, even which Paul himself taught (Acts 17:10-11). And it is recorded to the praise of the Church of Ephesus that they had tried them which said they were Apostles and were not, and had found them liars (Rev. 2:2). And indeed, it is verity that we ought to look for, and not suffer ourselves to be carried away with words and shows. For "whosoever is a good and true Christian," says St. Augustine, "must know that wheresoever he shall find truth, it belongs to his Lord"(Augustine, *de Dost Christ. 1. 2. Quisquis bomus verites, Christianus est, Domini sui esse intelligat, ubicunq, invenerit veritatem.*).

Let us therefore search into this truth so that we may find out the true Church where salvation is to be had.

The Greek word is ἐκκλησία; it signifies *a company, an assembly,* or congregation of people called together, and is sometimes taken for civil meetings in towns and cities or human societies (Acts 19:32), sometimes for ecclesiastical assemblies and meetings of the Church and people of God, as in our text and everywhere in Scripture and ecclesiastical writers. It is also vulgarly used for the place where the congregation meets to perform religious service, but improperly and abusively, and is therefore reprehended by *Laurentius Valla*, "Many," he says, "called sacred temples by the name of the Church, but I know not by what right, for indeed the word doth signify a congregation of men, not places," (Valla *l. 4. c. 47. Mulei Ecclesia, nescio quo jure, ades sacras oppillant, cum caetum hominii figusicoi, non loca.*). Which I would entreat you to note, because our adversaries, in their *Rhemes Testament*, do with such spiteful words traduce us for translating "Congregation," rather than "Church." They would make the world believe, with their *Bragadochio Campian*, that the very name of the Church is a scarecrow to Protestants (*cf.* Rhem. on Eph. 5:23 *ch. 3. Audito jun Eccle. Sic nomine, hostis expallise*).

They might have moderated their sharp censure, considering that the translation was answerable to the propriety of the Greek word; or they might have opened their eyes and looked into our Book of Articles, published twenty years before their Rhemes Notes did see the light (1562); or they might have seen, if they had not been willfully blind, that in our Book of Common Prayer, the word *Church* is ordinarily used in every passage: in our prayers, in the administration of the Sacraments, in the celebration of matrimony, in the confession of our Faith, at every meeting of the Church. By all which evidences, it may appear how far the Church of England is from any distaste of the name of the Church. But indeed they had their answer long ago, that their note is false and foolish, and that "the translator rather used the word "Congregation," than "Church," to avoid ambiguity; but after the people were taught to distinguish of the word "Church," and to understand it for the mystical Body of Christ, the later translators used that term, not that the other was any corruption, or the later any correction, but to declare that both is one," (*cf.* Dr. Fulke against Rhemes).

  Let us leave the meaning of the word and come to the thing and matter itself. The Church, out of which there is no salvation, is set forth unto us in a diverse notion: not that there is any more than one true Church, but because that one Church is considered in a diverse respect, and is in the parts of it a different condition. The name of the Church comprehends sometimes the whole company and congregation of the faithful, that ever were, are, or shall be to the end of the world, (see Augustine in *Psa. 56 Qui fuerunt ante nos, & future sunt post nos, usq. Ad finem seculi.*). Within this notion are included not only that part which is militant in earth, but also that which is triumphant in heaven, yes, the very angels themselves

(Augustine, *Enchir.* c. 55. *Templum Dei est Ecclesia Sancta, sc. Universa inc aelo & in terra*). Therefore, it is said that by Christ, God has reconciled "all things unto himself, and set at peace, through the *blood* of his cross, both the things in earth, and the things in heaven," (Col 1:20). These are the elect, invisible, known only to God in the judgment of verity and certainty (Eph. 1:4, 1 Pet. 1:2); "The Lord," the Apostle says, "knoweth who are his," (2 Tim. 2:19); and known to men only in the judgment of charity; as we may see by the same Apostle to the Thessalonians, distinguishing the sound members of the Church from the counterfeit; "But we ought to give thanks always for you, brethren, beloved of the Lord, because that God hath from the beginning chosen you to salvation," (2 Thess. 2:13; Rom. 2:28-29).

In a second notion, by "the Church" is understood the society of those which make external profession of the truth, being a mixed company, consisting of good and bad. And in this acceptation, it is taken sometimes for the general company of professed Christians, living in any one or more ages (Matt. 22:10): so we call the prime Christians in the Apostles' time, and the near adjoining ages, in which the assemblies continued orthodox and sound in the faith, the primitive Church. Sometimes also the name "Church" is given to particular congregations, being members of the universal, as the Church of Rome, the Church of Corinth, the Church of

Ephesus, and the like. Again, in particular Churches, the name of the Church is sometimes given to the Pastors, as where our Savior says, "Tell it unto the Church," (Matt. 18:17). Sometimes to the people, as may appear by Saint Paul's charge given to the elders of the Church of Ephesus, "Take heed," he says, "unto yourselves, and to all the flock, whereof the Holy Spirit hath made you Overseers, to feed the Church of God, which he hath purchased with his own blood," (Acts 20:28). Sometimes the name "Church" includes both pastors and people, as in the Revelation, where it is said, "To the seven Churches, which are in Asia," (Rev. 1:4, 20), is meant both the angels or ministers of those Churches and the candlesticks or Churches themselves, as afterwards it is expounded; in this sense it is so often said, "Let him that hath an ear, hear what the Spirit says to the Churches," (Rev. 2:7, *etc.*). These distinctions, as hereafter we shall see, are of great use for the clearing of many necessary truths.

And first of all, from hence we may derive the true definition of the Church, where they must be united that ever looked to be saved. It is out of all controversy that such must be the number of the elect (according to the first notion of the Church) as hath been shown before, upon the point of election, being the first grace, and fountain of all other graces accompanying salvation. But yet, because the elect are not subject to the eyes of men, but are only known to God, the sacred Scriptures direct us everywhere to the visible Church, according to the second notion: for whomsoever God does elect to the end, those he appoints to the means tending to that end.

Such therefore as desire salvation, must join themselves to the visible Church, by the ordinary way and means of effectual calling, justification, and sanctification; all which graces express themselves visibly to the eye of the world, by their effects and properties, causing the faithful to shine as a light in a dark place.

Let us come then to the definition of the visible Church: which I cannot better commend to you, than in the words of our Church of England; and it is this, "The visible Church of Christ, is a congregation of faithful men, in the which, the pure Word of God is preached, and the sacraments be duly ministered, according to Christ's Ordinance, in all those things that of necessity are requisite to the same," (*Thirty-Nine Articles of the Church of England*, Article 19).

Where we have the essential parts of a true definition: namely, the general and common matter, of which the Church is materially constituted; in these words, "A congregation of faithful men." And the difference, by which the Church is formally distinguished from all other societies, partly in the former words, partly in these words following, *viz.* "In which the pure Word of God is preached, and the Sacraments duly ministered, *etc.*"

To open the definition distinctly and plainly, we call the Church "A congregation of faithful men," to distinguish it both from civil and profane societies, that are without, as also from hypocrites and unsound members that are within the Church, but not of it.

Again, we say, that the Church "is a congregation of faithful men, in which the pure Word of God is preached, and the sacraments duly ministered, according to Christ's ordinance;" to distinguish the Orthodox and true Church from heretical assemblies, which maintain doctrine against the foundation; as also from idolatrous and superstitious societies, who do not serve God aright, according to his will revealed in his Word, but after the inventions and traditions of men: concerning whom, Christ alleging the Prophet says, "In vain they do worship me, teaching for doctrines the commandments of men," (Isa. 29:13; Matt. 15:9).

We add further, "in all those things that of necessity are requisite to the same," both to meet with will-worshipers, as also with schismatic conventicles, who make every external and indifferent ceremony an essential part of the worship of God, and therefore fly the assemblies of the most orthodox Churches for such external rites, as if they were gross idolaters, and not lawfully to be communicated with it.

From this definition in this way explained, we gather three remarkable points, carefully to be noted of all, that laying aside all prejudice and partiality, desire to be rightly informed in what Church they may find salvation.

1. That it is wherever the society of the faithful may be found, and is not alleged or tied to any one particular place or person.

2. That it is to be discerned from all others by the purity and soundness of doctrine; and by the due administration of the sacraments.

3. That it admitted nothing as of the necessity to salvation, or as an absolute and necessary part of worship, that is not consonant to the Word of God, according to Christ's ordinance in the same.

Touching the first point, that wherever the society of the faithful is, there is the true visible Church, and is not locally or personally tied to any. Let St. Peter, the prime bishop of Rome, as they call him, determine it, "Of a truth," he says, "I perceive, that God is no accepter of persons: but in every nation, he that feareth him, and worketh righteousness, is accepted with him," (Acts 10:34-35). Here is no one Africa, in it no one Cartenna, no one person or order of Bishops, where unto the Church should be tied. Here is no Italy, no one Rome, no one Pope or succession of Popes, challenging an allegation or dependence of all Churches upon it. But where *true faith and the fear of God is*, there is the Church of Christ.

This was revealed to St. John in a vision, where we may see that the Church is the company of "the redeemed, out of every kindred, and tongue, and people, and nation," (Rev. 5:9). He received no revelation concerning any one eminent place above all others, upon which all other Churches and their members should depend, as their oracle. Only this was showed unto him by vision, that "that great City, which then reigned over the Kings of the earth [and that we know was Rome]," was resembled to a woman, called "the great whore," by whom the kings and inhabitants of the earth have been made "drunk with the wine of her fornication," (Rev. 17:1-2, 18). If our Romanists like this, let them take it and make much of it, we do not envy them.

When the Apostles converted any to the faith, did they direct them to any particular country, city, or Church of note, and namely, to Rome, as whereunto they must of necessity be united, or else there was not salvation for them? If a man in this case of conscience, being troubled in mind, should demand of a Jesuit or seminary what he should do to attain everlasting life, his answer would readily be this, "You must be reconciled to the Church of Rome." But if St. Paul were asked the same question, as sometime he was by the jailer, what would be his answer? Surely none other than but this,

"What must thou do to be saved? Believe on the Lord Jesus Christ, and thou shalt be saved, and thy house," (*cf.* Acts 16:30-31).

When so many souls, with pricked and perplexed hearts, cried out to the Apostles, "Men and brethren, what shall we do?" Did St. Peter salve their sore consciences with the blame of reconciliation to Rome? No, no: Rome had then no Christian being; but he united them to the Church of the faithful, by calling them to repentance and faith, and to enter into the Church by baptism. "Repent," he says, "and be baptized every one of you, in the name of Jesus Christ," (Acts 2:37-38). The visible Church then, where whosoever will be saved must be reconciled, is the Congregation of the faithful, of what nation, or country, or condition no matter who they are, "for," says the Apostle, "there is neither Jew nor Greek, there is neither bond nor free, there is neither male nor female: for ye are all one in Christ Jesus," (Gal. 3:28). Wherefore, our blessed Lord hath left us in this case a sure rule and stay, whereupon the Christian soul may safely rest, and it is this, "Where two or three," he says, "are gathered together in my name, there am I in the midst of them," (Matt. 18:20).

Absurdly, therefore, have the Romish faction coined a new definition of the Visible Church, wherein they make the most formal and essential part to be this, namely, to be under the regiment of one head and governor of the Universal

Church, the *Vicar of Christ on Earth*, and St. Peter's *Successor* to wit, the Bishop of Rome, so that without adherence to, and dependence on this head, they admit no man to salvation.

The grossness of this conceit may appear by these *evidences*:

1. To define the Church in this manner, as they do, is most illogical and unreasonable. For a true and perfect definition requires that it be constituted solely of causes materially and formally essential unto the thing defined; so that the one can never exist without the other. But it is far otherwise with the true visible Church: for that was both, and might be defined, and thousands of souls united unto it, and saved in it, before ever the Church of Rome had any being in the world, as hath been shown before in part. How many famous Churches were planted by the Apostles that never cast the glance of an eye towards Rome? – as Corinth, Galatia, Ephesus, and the rest of the Seven Churches of Asia? How many thousands of souls converted, that never heard of any such universal head, or so much as the name of Rome? And indeed what should be allowed, but that they may be saved without any such respect, which have the graces of faith and repentance, and are entered by baptism, to which the promise is made in the general commission (Acts 2:28). "Go ye," our Lord says, "into all the world, and preach the Gospel to every creature: He that believeth, and is baptized, shall be saved,"

(Mark 16:15-16). Again, if there were such necessity to be united to the *See of Rome*, on pain of damnation, how did it come to pass that St. Cyprian (as our Adversaries themselves confess) in a council of fourscore and seven bishops, opposed himself against the Pope, and being cut off from communion with that great heathen, yet died a blessed saint, and was honored with the crown of martyrdom, dying out of that communion and, as Bellarmine says, never found to make any retraction?

Or, if to adhere to this one universal head is a matter of so great consequence as they make it—that the salvation of all men depend on it—is it credible that it should be so unknown to Gregory the Great, that he himself being bishop of Rome above five hundred years after Christ, should renounce it with so many titles of disgrace in one epistle? He calls it "a name of novelty, an impious name, a title of singularity," and that "he which taketh it upon him is the forerunner of the Antichrist;" with many more disgraceful terms given to that proud and pompous title elsewhere. Besides, how can that be a perpetual and essential part of the Church's definition which was not known in the Christian world so many hundred years after Christ. But as their own learned historians confess, was obtained of Phocas the Emperor, by Boniface the third, who was the second Pope, that succeeded after St. Gregory? "Boniface the third," says Platina, "obtained of Phocas the

Emperor with much importunity, that the seat of St. Peter should be described and taken of all, for the head of all Churches." Where, then, was this head before? St. Gregory himself will satisfy us. "None," he says, "of my predecessors, the bishops of Rome, did ever assume or challenge to himself the name of Universal Bishop." We see, then, how unreasonable it is that dependence on the *See of Rome* should be essential to the *definition* of the visible Church, and of necessity to salvation, as they would make their blindfold followers believe.

2. Again, it is manifest that, as St. Augustine speaks, "in those things that are plainly set down in Scripture, we may find whatsoever concerns faith and good life." Now let us search the whole *book* of God, from the first of Genesis, to the last of Revelation, and we shall not find so much as one word, either of prophesy, precept, promise, or precedent to countenance any such *necessary* adherence to Rome. How then can this be so main a point of faith, as the Romanists would have it, that has not so much as one express Scripture to ground itself on?

3. And is it indeed so weighty a point of Christian belief? In what creed, I pray, may we find it? I am sure it is not in the Apostles' Creed, unless they find it in some thirteenth new-coined article of their own.

There is only one Holy Catholic Church, the communion of Saints, which for the visible and militant part of it, is all one in effect with our definition, *viz.* That the visible Church is a congregation of faithful men; saints by calling, as St. Paul speaks. In the Nicene Creed, there is only added, by way of explication, the word "Apostolic," ("I believe in one Catholic and Apostolic Church") to show, against the heretics of that time, that that was the only true catholic and orthodox Church, which continued in the doctrine of the Apostles, as for Athanasius in his *Creed*, he makes catholic religion to consist in the true catholic faith and belief of those things that are of necessity to salvation, not alleging the believer to repose himself on any one place, as Rome, or Constantinople, or the like; but places him that shall be saved in the congregation of the faithful. And for good reason; for he knew well that Arianism had possessed all places, yes Rome itself, and had infected the head, even Liberius himself, the Bishop of Rome. This is not only witnessed by the Fathers, as Athanasius, Jerome, Hillary and Augustine, but is also acknowledged by their own Romish doctors, cardinals and historians, though Bellarmine and Baronius would gladly feign some excuse for him.

    4. Moreover, it must be considered, that Rome is, and ever was (when it was at the best) but a *particular* Church, and

member of the universal, as other Churches are: and therefore can no more challenge the dependence of other Churches on it, then they can subject it to any of them. See how clearly and fully St. Paul, writing to the Romans, speaks to this point: where, telling them that he had received "grace and Apostleship, for obedience to the faith, among all nations; among whom," he says, "ye are also the called of Jesus Christ," (Rom. 1:5-6). He does not say, above whom, as giving Rome primacy over all the rest, but "among whom," as conjoining them in fraternity with other Churches, and them with it.

5. Lastly, we must know that Rome is not only a particular Church, but is also subject to error, as well as other Churches. This the Apostle intimates by that severe caveat, which he gives to the Church of Rome, among other Gentiles, "Be not high minded," he says, "but fear. For if God spared not the natural branches, take heed, lest he also spare not thee. Behold therefore the goodness and severity of God; on them which fell, severity: but towards thee, goodness; if thou continue in his goodness: otherwise thou also shalt be cut off," (Rom. 11:20-22). Here we see that Rome has no more immunity from error than any other Church, no, no more than the Church of the Jews; Rome, no more than Jerusalem; and that God ties himself to none, but with condition; if they do answer his goodness to them, with perseverance and continuance in his goodness, and care of correspondent duty

to him. Therefore, our Church of England has well added in the Article of the Church, these words, *viz.* "As the Church of Jerusalem, Alexandria, and Antioch, have erred; so also the Church of Rome hath erred, not only in their living, and manner of ceremonies, but also in matters of faith," (*Article* 19).

THE ERRORS OF THE ROMAN CHURCH

Here it will not be amiss, out of the manifold errors of the Romish Church, to give instance in a few, as a taste of the rest. I will enroll them in a short catalogue, and they shall be only such as no man that will be a Roman Catholic, can avoid, but must on pain of damnation, in his order and place, believe and practice. The very naming of the errors may be a *sufficiet couictio*, they are so palpably gross.

1. They deny the reading of the holy Scriptures in common to Christian people; which is not only an error, but the cause of all other errors: as our Savior told the Sadducees, "Ye do err, not knowing the scriptures," (Matt. 22:29). And this they do, contrary to the express command of Christ, "Search the Scriptures," (John 5:39). This is contrary to the exhortation of St. Paul, "Let the Word of God dwell in you richly," (Col 3:16), contrary to the usual practice of the faithful in all antiquity, both Jews and Christians (Deut. 6:6 and 11:18;

Acts 17:11). This is also contrary to the very end and use for which Sacred Scriptures were written, as the Apostle tells the old Romans, "Whatsoever things," he says, "were written aforetime, were written for our learning, that we, through patience and comfort of the Scriptures, might have hope," (Rom. 15:4). Yes, and contrary to the general judgment of the Orthodox Fathers of the Church, "The Scripture being," as St. Gregory said well, "nothing else, but an Epistle of Almighty God to His creature."

2. They attribute such eminency of power to the Pope, over all souls subject to him, that in a blind-fold obedience they must be at his beck, to believe and to do as he will have them. Therefore they describe him, *The Supreme Judge in cases of faith and manner*; and do not say, it is *sufficient*, if he says the word. And they are so impatient of control in all this, that no man must dare to say to him, "*Curitafacis?* Why are you doing?" though this fact is odious to name. This is an error, not only impious in religion, but pernicious in any civil State. By this, not only his *probihet*, forbidding, shall keep men from God's true worship and service, but his commanding shall arm them against their sovereign; as we know, it has done here in England. Far were the greatest Apostles from assuming to themselves any such absolute power; their voice was, "Be ye followers of me, as I am of Christ," (1 Cor. 11:1). And again,

"Though we, or an Angel from heaven, preach any other Gospel unto you, let him be accursed." Therefore they must necessarily be strangely bewitched and possessed with error, that can believe that a sinful man should have a privilege above the Apostles and angels.

    3. Their whole fabric and form of religious service, and public worship of God, being in an unknown tongue to the people; what is it, but a notorious and intolerable error? For take to heart, I pray, and think seriously what a lamentable condition those people are in, that stand bound all the days of its life, to resort to a Church, where in their most solemn liturgies, masses, and service, they do not understand one sentence to their soul's comfort. The whole volume of sacred Scripture, and examples of both Testaments are against it. St. Paul in its confutation, bestows a large chapter, proving, that it is not only unfruitful, but *barbarous*, and a fearful note of God's judgment on a people (1 Cor. 14:11). They do not have an ancient Orthodox Father to father this error: among them you shall hear these voices sounding, "Let the Greeks in Greek, let the Romans in the Roman tongue, let all in their own language pray and praise God." Again, "How canst thou," St. Cyprian says, "desire to be heard of God, who doest not understand thyself?" No, our Christian reformed Churches have this happiness, that among the Romanists themselves, there are of chief note, those that ingenuously confess, that it

is better, and more edifying, that public prayers should be in the vulgar and common language, known of the people, than in Latin. Let us bless God then, that has vouchsafed us the better part, and pray that he would open their eyes, that are so blinded with error, that they may take part with us.

4. That foul error of idolatrous adoration of images, in common practice among them, how expressly contrary is it to the commandment of God? "Thou shalt not make to thyself any graven image, nor the likeness of anything...Thou shalt not bow down to them, nor worship them," (Exod. 20:4; Lev. 26:1). An error, of which they are so consciously guilty themselves, that in their catechisms, and confession of their penitents, they commonly *leave out* that Commandment. And their professors being charged with this error, are so ashamed of it, that they in plain terms deny that they do any such religious service to images; in which indeed denying their own religion, and incurring the curse of their Trent Council: which anathematizes all those that hold against their decree in this, namely, "That due honor and worship ought to be given to images," (Council. *Trid. De Image*). But does not their real practice cross their verbal excuse? For if they do not worship images, why do they perform so many religious services to them? They veil, and bow down to them, they set up before them lights in honor of them, they offer up incense and other sacrifices to them, they expand and spread forth their arms

before them in prayer. What can they do *more*, for *outward* service, to God himself? This idolatrous practice is not only condemned in sacred Scripture, as expressly as blasphemy, witchcraft, murder, adultery, or any other sin, and avoided of all the faithful of both Testaments; but is renounced as impious by the Fathers, for many ages after Christ; affirming images in the Church, to be contrary to the authority of the Scriptures: that there is no Religion where an image is. And St. Gregory, about 600 years after Christ, forbids utterly the adoration of images, only allowing the historical use of them, as we do at this day. By which we may see that this *soul* error had not as yet in so long time possessed the *See of Rome*.

5. Their priests in the Mass offer up a propitiatory sacrifice, both for the quick and the dead, and their blind followers are bound so to believe, and both pray and pay to be had in this memento. Where all propitiatory sacrifices have their end in Christ, who is the end of the Law, and the only Sacrificing Priest, in the Gospel, being a Priest forever, according to the order of Melchizedek. This Sacrifice is only *one*, and only *once* offered, and that by himself alone, and therefore is called "The offering of the body once for all: and this Man," says the Apostle, "after he had offered one sacrifice for sin, forever sat down at the right hand of God, for by one offering he hath perfected forever them that are sanctified,"

(Heb. 10:10, 12, 14). How sacrilegious then and blasphemous is that *daily* propitiatory sacrifice of theirs? Where is their warrant for it? Seeing Christ ordained no sacrifice to be offered by any sacrificing Priest, but only a sacrament, commemorative to be administered by the Pastors of the Church, and received together with them, by the people. Where, in the Gospel, can they find the calling of a Sacrificing Priest? The commission is only, "Go, teach and baptize;" and the subject of their teaching must be no other thing, but that which Christ has commanded. Other ordinary "Priesthoods" our Lord ordained none but Pastors and Teachers. The name "Sacrifice" we do not deny to the Sacrament, but with the Fathers, we call it a sacrifice for diverse good respects, and namely, because (as the *Master of Sentences* says, out of St. Augustine and St. Ambrose) it is the remembrance and representation of the true sacrifice, offered upon the Altar of the Cross. As for any proper, real, and propitiatory Sacrifice, we may see by this, that it was not known in Peter Lombard's time, about twelve hundred years after Christ, and therefore, is far from being truly Catholic.

6. Their transubstantiation, which they oblige every Christian soul to believe, not only on pain of their fagot fire, but of the fire of hell; that is, that after the words of consecration, there ceases to be the substance of bread and wine, and that there remain only the outward accidents, show

and shape of it; under which, the very body and blood of Christ is substantially and corporeally enclosed. How directly contrary is this to the express words of Christ, in the first institution? For our Lord Jesus, after the consecration and blessing, testifies the elements to remain in their substance, calling them by their right names, "bread," and "the fruit of the vine." The same St. Paul does, and that often in one short context (1 Cor. 11:26-28). It is an error, indeed against common sense, for the senses of sight, smell, taste, and feeling report, if there does not remain the substance of bread and wine after consecration. If a man has sufficient quantity of them, he may, for a proportionable time, sustain nature, with no other food; which could not be, if there remained nothing but the external accidents, and mere *show* of bread and wine. It is against the nature of a true body, which is, to be only in one place, at one time, and that in his due dimension and substance. Now we know and believe that Christ is true man, in all things the same to us, only sin excepted; and therefore to make him to be without dimension, is so many hundred, no thousands of places at one instant, manifestly implies a tacit denial of his human nature. It is against our Christian Creed, where we believe that Christ (leaving the world, in regard of his bodily presence) *ascended into heaven, and sits on the right hand of God, and from thence he shall come to judgment:* which St. Peter aptly interprets in these words; "Whom," he says, "the heaven must receive, until the times of restitution of all things," (Acts 3:21). But there is not one evidence more apparently convincing this error, than if we consider, that at the institution of the Sacrament, Christ sat visibly before the Apostles, that they might plainly see with their eyes where his true body was. And with it did expressly signify to them that he did not speak simply of his body, but of his body crucified, and blood shed; which as yet was not then done, "This," says our Lord Christ, "is my body, which is given for you," (Luke 22:19): or as St. Paul relates it, "which is broken for you," (1 Cor. 11:24). Again, of the cup, he says, "This is my blood of the new Testament, which is shed for many," (Matt. 26:28; Mark 14:24); adding also for the clearing of all doubt in this, the commemorative use of the Sacrament, which evidently confutes all carnal and corporeal presence, "This do," he says, "in remembrance of me," that is, *of me crucified*, "For," the Apostle says, "as often as you shall eat this bread, and drink this cup, ye shew forth the Lord's death til he come."

Now where he calls the bread his body, and the wine his blood, it is according to the usual manner of Scripture; speaking everywhere of *Sacraments*, he calls them by the name of those things of which they are, Sacraments. So circumcision was called *the covenant*, because it was the sign and seal of the covenant (Gen 17:10-11; Rom. 4:11). So the paschal lamb is called *the Passover*, because it was the sign of the Passover (Ex 12:11). It is said in the same sense by St. Paul, that the rock was Christ, because it typically and sacramentally represented Christ (1 Cor. 10:4). So the ancient Fathers spoke and thought of the Sacrament. "The Lord doubted not," says St. Augustine, "to say, this is my body, seeing he appointed it to be the sign of his body." Yet for as much as our Romish adversaries harden themselves in their error, on a conceit they have entertained that we hold the Sacraments to be only bare and naked signs. It must be known for their conviction, that it is but a mere slander, which they take to be true, on the bare report of their guides, without so much as either hearing or reading what we hold. The truth is, we hold no such thing, neither is the question between them and us, whether Christ is substantially present in the Sacrament, but *de modo*, concerning the manner of his presence. They say, by conversion of the bread into the very body of Christ: so that whosoever eats the consecrated bread, eats carnally the very body of Christ, whether it be man, beast, or vermin that eats. We, according both to Scripture and the Fathers, teach that Christ is *pabulum mentis, non dentis*, food for the mind, not for the mouth. And he is as truly received of every true believer, as the bread and wine itself. Our Church of England is in no point more clear and plain than in this, affirming that "such as rightly, worthily and with faith receive the same," partake of the body and blood of Christ. And with it determines *de modo & de medio*, both of the manner, and of the means, in these very words, "The body of Christ is given, taken, and eaten in the Supper, only after an heavenly and spiritual manner. And the means whereby the body of Christ is received and eaten in the Supper, is faith," (*Article* 28). Yes and Calvin himself, at whom their spite is most, and whom they most scandalize in this matter, so plainly delivers the truth in it, with us, that Bellarmine is constrained to confess, that Calvin teaches, "That the body of Christ is truly given unto us in the Supper. That our souls are fed with the substance of the body of Christ, and that it is not an empty and vain sign." But for the full conviction of this error, the novelty of it may be sufficient: for it is so far from any catholic antiquity, that Erasmus affirms transubstantiation to be but a late definition. And their own subtle Doctor Scotus said, that before the Council of Lateran it was *no Doctrine of faith*. Which was above twelve hundred years after Christ: for that Council was held in the year of our Lord, 1215.

    7. On the former error depends another, and that is the adoration of the consecrated Host or Eucharist. For on this false ground, that there remains no more substance of bread and wine, but the very body and blood of Christ by conversion, they prostrate themselves before it, and worship

it, as God himself, with that kind of religious worship, which they call *Latria*, peculiar only to God. And this they do, not only in the use of the Sacrament, at the elevation or lifting up of it by the Priest, to that very purpose: but to the same end, they make reservation of it, and use circumgestion, or carrying of it about in open shows and processions; contrary to the express institution of Christ, who ordained no Sacrament *extra usum*, or out of the use of it. Nor did he ever say, "This is my body. This is my blood," but with an *edite & bebite*, "Eat ye and drink ye:" so they that cannot pretend any bodily presence outside the use of the Sacrament. And in it, as has been shown before, there is no conversion, or transubstantiation. And therefore, the adoration must necessarily determine and rest in the creature: and so is none other but a mere *artolatry*, or bread worship, and abominable idolatry. The heathen could say, "who is so mad, as to believe that to be God, which he eats?" And indeed this madness has made the heathen abhor Christian religion, and in contempt of it to say, "seeing Christians eat the God whom they worship, let my soul be with the philosophers."

  8. Their private, or solitary Mass, in which the Priest only participates, the people as in a theater gazing and looking on. This they so highly extoll, and make the most eminent part of their religion, and public service. Consider it

seriously, and we shall find it without all ground and warrant in God's Word, no, *ex diametro,* directly *adverse and opposite to Christ's ordinance.* For our Lord, in the Supper did ordain a communion of many together, not a solitary eating and drinking of one alone by himself. His mandate is, "Take ye, eat ye, drink ye all of it," (Matt. 26:26-27). And St. Paul accordingly calls the Sacrament, the "communion in the blood of Christ," (1 Cor. 10:16-17). This yields a reason, from the correspondence between the elements and the communicants. "For" he says, "we, being many, are one bread and one body: for we are all partakers of that one bread." And this goodly Mass is so far from having any acquaintance with antiquity, excepting only the name, that it was not known in St. Gregory's time, so many hundred years after Christ. For then the voice of the deacon openly in the Church was this, "Whosoever doth not communicate, let him depart."

9. Their dry diet, in the Sacrament of the Lord's Supper. In which they deprive the people of the cup, how sacrilegious is it, and injurious to the people in the prime institution, our blessed Lord gave this express charge, "Drink ye all of it," (Matt. 26:27). And St. Mark notes their answerable obedience. "And they all," he says, "drank of it," (Mark 14:23). And St. Paul faithfully reporting the institution, and according to the practice of the Church, often repeats as well the receiving of the wine, as of the bread by the people.

And so he exhorts, "Let a man," he says, "examine himself, and so let him eat of this bread and drink of this cup." Here, we may see, was no dry feast. Here was no lame Sacrament, like theirs, hopping upon one leg. No, it is a truth so evident, that it is by their own Cassander ingenuously confessed, "that for the space of a thousand years since Christ," in the "Roman Church itself, it was ordinarily dispensed to every member of the Church in both kinds. And that," he says, "by the testimonies of innumerable Ancients, both Greek and Latin," (Cassan. *Consult. Art.* 22.).

10. Their invocation of Saints, offering up unto them as solemn and set prayers, as to the sacred Deity itself, what is it, but a manifest derogation, and robbing of God, even of his particular right, which is, to be the sole hearer of the prayers of his creatures? "O thou," says the Psalmist, "that hearest prayer, unto thee shall all flesh come," (Psa. 65:2). For we must know that it is the act of an infinite majesty, at one instant to hear the manifold variety of petitions of all men upon the face of the earth, yea and to know the very thoughts and desires of every heart, prayer being principally the act of the heart. Upon this very ground wise Solomon takes for granted that all prayer ought to be made to God only, "Hear thou in heaven," he says to God, "thy dwelling place, and forgive, and do, and give to every man according to his ways, whose heart thou knowest: for thou, even thou only knowest

the hearts of all the Children of men," (1 Kings 8:39). Again, prayers to Saints lack that threefold prop that must support every true and acceptable service to God, that is to say, *precept*, *promise*, and *pattern*. For invocation of God's name, we have express commandment, "Call upon me," (Psa. 50:15). And our Savior commands that when we pray, we should direct our prayers to "Our Father in heaven," (Luke 11:2). We have also a sure word of promise, "Whatsoever ye shall ask the Father in my name, he will give it to you," (John 16:23). And, "Whosoever shall call upon the name of the Lord shall be saved," (Rom. 10:13). We have no such precept, no such promise, to warrant and encourage us to invocate the Blessed Virgin, St. Peter, St. Paul, or any or all of the Saints. Again, for prayer to God only, we have express pattern, both personal, in all the fathers from the first Adam, in the Patriarchs, Prophets, Apostles, and prime Orthodox Fathers of the Church, who suffered martyrdom for this very point, that God only in Christ is to be adored, and called upon (Gen. 4:26; Psa. 22:4-5; Eph. 3:14; Phil. 4:6). We have also a real pattern, in that heavenly manual of prayer and praise, *the Sacred Psalter*, or Psalms of David: together with the set forms of the faithful prayers recorded everywhere in Scripture, and all directed to God only, not on a pattern of prayer to saints. This is ingenuously confessed by their own Eccius and other

Pontificians, that invocations of Saints have *no warrant* in sacred Scripture; not in the Old Testament, because the Fathers were then in Limbo, nor in the New Testament, lest the Gentiles should return again to their old Idol worship; and lest the Apostles should be charged with arrogance, as bespeaking beforehand their own glory, and worship to be done to themselves after their death. No more, they confess, that it is the safer and better way to call on God *only in the name of Jesus Christ*. And one of them, out of a work ascribed to St. Augustine, concludes the question this way, "More safely and more sweetly do I speak, in prayer to my Jesus, than to any of the saints."

The story of George, Duke of Saxony is memorable here. Lying on his deathbed, the monks like locusts swarming about him, and beholding his agony, exhorted him; one, to invocate the Virgin Mary; another, to pray to these and these Saints, for help in that extremity. But a Nobleman, one of his familiars, standing by, directed his speech to the Duke in this manner, "Your Highness," he says, "was accustomed in your politic affairs, to take up this proverb: *To go the direct way, without circumstances, is the most compendious course.*" Why then should your Highness, in this most dangerous passage, go about the furthest way, and not rather go the direct way to God himself by Christ, who both will and can certainly help?

Erasmus among others of his pleasant conceits, merrily glances at this error, reporting a story of one at sea, where (as their manner is) every man in a wreck, flies to his personal saint, as if it were his *tutelar god*. There was one, he says, among the rest, when he saw the present and imminent danger, and that there was no delaying; in the midst of this distraction, thought with himself, if I should pray to St. Nicholas, it is uncertain whether he hears me, and it may be he is busy in hearing and dispatching other petitioners; or if it is not so, yet it may be that he cannot have so speedy access to God, to mediate for me, as my present necessity requires. I will therefore, he says, take the safest and surest course, and go the direct way to God himself, by Christ, because it is written in the Psalm, "Call on me in the day of trouble, I will deliver thee, and thou shalt glorify me," (Psa. 50:15). And in the Hebrews, "Let us therefore come boldly unto the Throne of Grace, that we may obtain mercy, and find grace to help in time of need," (Heb. 4:16). If any stumbles at this, that some fathers are alleged to countenance this error, let him remember that of St. Augustine, ""We must not hearken to, this say I, this say you," but this says the Lord." And distinctly, *first of himself*, he says, "I would not have you follow my authority, that you should therefore think anything necessary to be believed, because I say it. And of other fathers, what they held, may appear by that which he writes of St. Cyprian's epistle, *viz.* that it has no authority to bind him. "For," he says, "I do not hold St. Cyprian's letters to be canonical scripture, but I examine them by the canonical: and what I find thereunto agreeable, I embrace with his praise; what is not consonant, by his leave, I will leave. This is the true profession of a doctor, concerning the Scriptures, at his inauguration!" If any harp on the long custom of this error in the Christian world, let him consider, as one says well, that Christ did not say, "I am custom," but, "I am truth." And that custom without truth is but an old error, or, the antiquity of error. Which, like an old sore, is so much the worse, and more incurable, the older it is.

11. The prayer for the dead, to deliver them out of that fearful and hell-like torment in Purgatory, in which they are made to believe they lie boiling as in a fiery furnace: what an antithesis and plain opposition is there between the Word of truth and this gross error? We know, and are assured by the Word of God, "that the blood of Jesus Christ cleanseth and purgeth us from all sin," (1 John 1:7). So that there is no need of human purgatives either for venial sins, or for temporal punishment of sins mortal. For our Lord Jesus assured the faithful departing this life, that he that hears his word and believeth is "passed from death unto life," (John 5:24). And that they that die in the Lord are in a blessed estate and rest from their labors (Rev. 14:13). Yes, the poorest Lazarus that

dies in the faith of Abraham, is immediately in his precious soul conveyed by the angels into *Abraham's bosom (i.e. heaven)*, there possessed of heavenly joy, not afflicted with hellish torment. This may be a sufficient conviction of this error, that there is not one sentence, not one word, not one syllable, not one letter in the whole volume of Canonical Scripture, favoring *prayer for the dead*, as being in any such misery after their departure: nay, that there is express Scripture to the contrary. The Fathers were far from any such conceit, who held that the faithful deceasing are in a blessed condition, having obtained their desired end of victory, and beholding the Lord Jesus face to face. And that the friends of the deceased, counting him happy, gave thanks to the Author of the victory with a song. See here the difference between the ancient Fathers, and the now Romanists. They held the deceased faithful in a blessed and joyful estate—these count them to be in misery and torment. They congratulated their happiness. These condole their torments. They gave thanks for their attained victory—these pray and pay to free them out of their conceited captivity. In a word, they did sing for joy—these howl and cry for doleful sorrow.

12. Their daily devotions, which we see in their primers, rosaries, and manuals, what are they for the most part but leaders of blind superstition? For besides that they are, in most passages, directed to a wrong object, worshiping

the creature instead of the creator, and so changing, as St. Paul says, "the truth of God into a lie," (Rom. 1:25); they have with it this soul blot of superstitious vanity, that where God will be served by weight, they serve him by number: whereas he requires serious, weighty, and judicious devotions, framed according to our present wants, as we may see in the religious prayers of the Saints in Holy writings (1 Kings 8:38); they, directed by their blind guides, (like a horse in the mill) perform a superficial, slight, and circular service, placing virtue, and religious effect in the very number of their prayers, in saying so many times over a certain number of *Pater-nosters*, *Ave-Maries*, *Credoes* and the like. Read their books, and they will tell you that for three *Ave-Maries*, said three times over every day, at three several hours, and at every hour thrice, is granted three hundred days of pardon. Again, for saying before the image of five *Pater-nosters*, five *Aves* and a *Credo*, are granted thirty two thousand, seven hundred and fifty-five years of pardon. A multitude of these sopperies you may find everywhere in their superstitious devotions. And to further these numeral prayers, there was at the last found out a new trickle, the invention of beads. "When men," says Polidor Virgil, "began to number and reckon their prayers, as though God were in our debt, for often begging of him, there were devised by one Petrus Heremita, a Frenchman, certain beads, about the year of our Lord, 1090." The novelty of this *superstition* is conviction sufficient. But the shame of it is, that in the judgment of him that cannot err, it is so far from Christian piety, that it is no better than flat Heathenism. Therefore, our Savior, on that very ground, warns all Christians to avoid such vain repetitions. "When ye pray," he says, "use not vain repetitions, as the Heathen do: for they think that they shall be heard for their much speaking," which is, we see, in the Lord's account, but vain babbling (Matt. 6:7). A lively pattern of a Papist and a Protestant, for the manner of religious devotion, we may see in the priest of Baal and the prophet Elias paralleled together; the one continue from morning until noon, and from noon until evening, with "*Audinos, Audinos, O Baal, hear us, O Baal, hear us, etc.*" with much cursitation, and stirring, as the Romish fashion is: the other, that is, the good prophet Elias, a true pattern of piety, and sound religion, reverently and humbly addresses himself to call on God, praying in a short, but yet a sweet and heavenly manner, according to the present occasion. Read the story, and admire the difference (1 King 18:26-37).

To be brief: concerning auricular confession, that is, that every man do confess all his mortal sins, with all the circumstances, once every year at the least, and that privately to a Priest, at the least in vote or desire, yes, and that also of necessity to salvation; it is utterly without either rule or example of God's Word; and this want of Divine authority is ingenuously confessed by many of their own authors. The confessions we find in Scripture are either unto God only; or if unto men or before men, it was in these cases:

1. Before baptism, at the entrance into Christianity; as in those that were baptized by John the Baptist.

2. In a case of free and voluntary testfication of their sound conversion, as it is said in the Acts, "Many that believed came and confessed, and shewed their works," (Acts 19:18).

3. In case of some grievous sin, lying heavy on the conscience, as in the example of David's confession to Nathan the prophet (2 Sam 12:13).

4. In case of public scandal, to give glory to God, and satisfy the congregation, as in the example of Achan (Josh 7:19).

5. In the case of private injury done by one man to another, whether Priest or private man, as it is in St. James, "Confess your faults one to another, and pray one for another," (James 5:16).

In all these we have not one confession, after the Romish stamp, to be made of necessity to a Priest of all sins, and that anniversary, at the least once a year.

13. Their placing of religion in the distinction of meats, St. Paul has branded with the note of error, doctrine of devils, and deep hypocrisy, prophetically foretelling it to be a mark of

that Antichristian Apostasy that should befall these later times, "Now the Spirit," he says, "speaks expressly, that in the later times some shall depart from the faith, giving heed to seducing spirits, and doctrines of devils: speaking lies in hypocrisy, having their conscience seared with a hot iron; forbidding to marry, and commanding to abstain from meats, which God hath created to be received with thanksgiving, of them which believe and know the truth," (1 Time 4:1-3).

14. Their violent laying hands on themselves, by whippings, to make satisfaction, and procure acceptance with God, hath no ground in sacred Scripture, *unless they think the example of those priests of Baal a good warrant*. Indeed, I must necessarily say, they went beyond our Romanists; for they used knives and lances, these but whips; they lanced, but these lashed.

15. Their *extreme unction*, with which they shut up and end their Romish race in this world, is just as unwarrantable. For where they have but two only texts for it, they both fail them, as their own doctors ingenuously confess. Those Scriptures in St. Mark and St. James speak only of anointing with oil, for the miraculous curing of the sick (Mark 6:13; James 5:14); but they use anointing to no such end, but only when men are irrecoverable, and ready to depart out of this life. These instances may be sufficient for a taste of Romish

errors, being the most usual, and common to everyone that will be a professed Roman Catholic.

DEFINITIONS OF THE CHURCH

So we have opened the first branch of our definition of the Church, showing that the true Church is the company of the faithful, of what nation or country soever, and that it is not tied to any person or place, not to Rome; because many thousands were saved that never knew it, and before ever it was Christian. Rome's authority over others is in no Scripture, in no Creed. It is but a particular Church, and member only of the Universal, as others are, and subject to error as well as others.

The second branch of the definition of the Church is that it is discerned from all other societies by *soundness of doctrine*, and *due administration of the Sacraments*.

TRUE AND FALSE DOCTRINE

Touching doctrine, it is the earmark of Christ's sheep, "My sheep hear my voice," (John 10:27). It is that where the faithful are directed to try the true pastor from the impostor, the orthodox from the heretical. "Ye shall know them by their fruits," (Matt. 7:16). Therefore, St. John counsels, "not to believe every spirit, but to try the spirits, whether they are of God," (1 John 4:1); and charges the elect Lady and her children in this way, "If there come any unto you, and bring you not this doctrine, receive them not into your house, neither bid him, God speed," (2 John 10). And this charge he grounded on a Divine rule of *trial* in the word immediately going before. The rule is this, "Whosoever trangresseth, and abideth not in the doctrine of Christ, hath not God: he that abideth in the doctrine of Christ. He hath both the Father and the Son," (verse 9). And lest any should think it strange, that the trial of doctrine should be required of private Christians, our Savior puts it out of doubt; showing not only that it is and ought to be so, but directs how it may be done. For, having said, "My doctrine is not mine, but his that sent me," (John 7:16), he gives them a double rule, which being observed, they may discern of *doctrine*. The one concerns the hearer, the other the teacher. The rule concerning the hearer is this, "If any man will do his will, he shall know of the doctrine, whether it is of God, or whether I speak of myself." That is, *If a man in humility and sincerity of heart seeks to be informed in the truth,* and as God from time to time shall reveal it to him, makes the conscience put in practice that doctrine which he shall hear. And as Thophylact says, "Shall embrace virtue, and not suffer himself to be a slave to envy," and hate truth before he knows it; *such man shall be able to discern of doctrine*; but yet with this *proviso*, which there Theophylact inserts well, viz., "That this is one main part of doing the will of God; namely, to search the prophets and the Scriptures."

Touching the second rule, which concerns the Teacher, it is this, "He that speaks of himself, seeketh his own glory: but he that seeketh his glory that sent him, the same is true," (John 7:18). A good parallel, distinguishing exactly the false teacher from the true; the one seeking his own, the other God's glory. By this rule, we desire all men sincerely and without prejudice, to judge between us and our Roman adversaries. Look with an indifferent and impartial eye into the doctrine and practice on both parts. You shall find that all their doctrines and courses, in which they differ from us, aim altogether at the extolling of nature, man's works and merits, with a glance still at the magnifying and enriching of their Roman Synagogue. Where we, with our blessed Lord, make the scope of all our teaching and practice, *the glory of God*, and the praise of the all-sufficient merits of Christ.

This direction of our Savior is sufficient alone of itself to prove that the doctrine is the right trial of the Church, and its pastors. But besides, we find the congregation of the faithful described in the Acts of the Apostles, by this very note, that "they continued steadfastly in the Apostle's doctrine," (Acts 2:42). And the Thessalonians are commended, that they received the Word of God, not as the word of man; resting on the bare authority of the teacher, but, "as it is in truth, the Word of God," (1 Thess. 2:13). They that rested on men, under the name and color of the Church, and chief governors of the Church, the chief priests and elders of the people, did crucify Christ: whereas they that examined the doctrine by the Word of God, believed (Matt. 27:1). If therefore, you will approve yourselves to be the disciples of the Gospel, that is, true Christians, you must walk, Athanasius says, "by the rule of the Scriptures." It is sound doctrine, then, grounded on the Word of God, that the Christian should, rather *must* rest on, for the discerning of the *true Church*. For, whether it is concerning Christ, or concerning his Church, St. Augustine says, or touching any other thing pertaining to faith and life; "If we, or an Angel from heaven teach any otherwise, then that which ye have received in the Scriptures, let him be accursed." As for the Sacraments, that they are also discerning notes of the Church, I need here to say nothing, in regard that it has been sufficiently shown before, that they are so peculiar to the Church, that the one cannot be without the other.

THE THIRD BRANCH OF THE DEFINITION OF THE CHURCH

Concerning the third branch of the definition of the Church, that it admits nothing as necessary to salvation, or as an absolute part of God's worship, that is not according to the Word and ordinance of Christ. This fully completes and perfects the definition of the Church, which must be as pure in her religion, and worship, as she is found in her doctrine. That there be no mixture of man's invention with God's ordinance; for in the service of God, the hypothesis, or conditions of the prophet may ever hold good, "If the Lord is God, follow him: but if Baal, then follow him," (1 King 18:27). God will have *all or none*. He cannot abide that his fear, that is, his religious worship, should be taught by the precepts of men (Isa. 29:13), and therefore accounts it vain worship, and mere lost labor, when the commandments of men are taught for doctrines, and, as it were, rules, and principles of necessity to be observed (Matt. 15:9). This must be seriously considered, for better meeting with the two adversaries, which assail truth on both sides, with their different extremes. The one is the Romanist, who holds that the ceremonies of the Church may not be omitted, without grievous sin, inasmuch as they have spiritual virtue, and are parts of divine worship, and withal are meritorious (Bellarmine, *de Sacara*. 1.2 6.30). And they futher this conceit on the power which they attribute to the Church, to institute *jus jure*; that is, by her own right, such ceremonies: and therefore to make their followers pliable, they teach them as a main principle of their religion that they must obey with equal respect, in regard of salvation, the Mother's precept, as well as the Father's mandate: but they never consider, that the true Church is an obedient wife, and will not in anything contradict the will of her heavenly Spouse (Eph. 5:24).

    The second sort of adversaries are our separatists, who for every external and indifferent ceremony, make as great combustion and stir in the Church of God, as if some main Article of Faith were called in question. They must be entreated to consider that the Text does not simply condemn all commandments of men, but when they are taught for doctrines, and rules of God's worship, as Calvin speaks (Calvin, on *Matthew 5*); the doctrine of our Church might give them content, being the same with all the rest of the reformed Churches, namely, "That it is not lawful for the Church to ordain anything contrary to God's written Word: and that besides the same, it ought not to enforce anything to be believed for necessity of salvation," (Article 20). By which they may, if they will open their eyes without prejudice, see of what nature the ceremonies of our Church of England are. And so much for the definition of the Church; by which we may see what that Church is to which we must be joined, if ever we look for salvation; that is, the society of true believers.

THE STATE OF THE CHURCH

But for the better understanding of the state of the Church, diverse things are to be considered, which give more light to the doctrine, and more full satisfaction to such as desire unfeignedly to know the truth in this.

The first consideration is that the Church is only *one*; though different in time; as different as from the beginning to the end of the world; and in place, as remote as east from west, north from south; no, heaven from earth. Distinct for people, being of all countries and nations. For, as has been said before, "It is the society or congregation of the faithful of all ages." This unity of the Church is noted in the one Ark of Noah (Gen 6); in Solomon's Dove, "My dove, my undefiled, is but one," (Song 6:9): in the wheat field, in the draw net (Matt. 13:24,47; Luke 12:32); in one flock (Luke 12:32), one fold, under one shepherd (John 10:16): in one bridegroom (John 3:29): in one body, united to one Head, Christ, "For," the Apostle says, "by one Spirit are we all baptized into *one* body," (1 Cor. 12:13). This consideration seconds that which has been said of the Church; for it evidently evidences, and proves, that there is no necessity of being united to this or that particular Church, as Rome, or the like, so long as a man is of the number of the faithful, wheresoever dispersed; for, as St. Paul disputes, "The body is not one member, but many. Is the foot not of the body, because it is not the hand? Or the ear, because it is not the eye?" (1 Cor. 12:14-16). So we may truly say, is this or that National or Provincial Church, no Church, because it is not dependent on Rome? Are they that are baptized into one body, and united to Christ Jesus by one faith unfeigned, not members of the mystical Body of Christ, the Church, because they are not incorporated and reconciled to Rome? If the body, though it is but one, yet is not one member, but many. Then reason will teach us that every member has his proportionable nutriment, life, and motion from the head, without any dependence of one on another.

The second consideration is that it is Catholic or Universal; and that, in respect of time, place, and persons; because there is, ever was from the beginning, and ever shall be to the end of the world, a company, more or less, of true believers: because the Church is not confined within the limits of any one country, as in the time of the Jews, but is spread over the whole world: and because it consists of all sorts of degrees of men; "of all nations, kindreds, people and tongues," as it is in Revelation 7:9. So that to be of the Catholic Church, is to hold and believe as the Church as the

Church of the whole world ever did, and constantly holds and believes. Therefore it was, that in the ancient Church, when heresies and schisms sprang up, those that held to the truth, had given to them the name of *Catholic*, for their communion with the Church of the whole world; not for their communion with this or that particular Church. While the Romish Church assumes the title of "The Catholic Church;" calling itself *Catholicam Apostolicam Romanam* , being as other Churches, but a particular Church; what it does, but expose itself to the laughter of the whole world? For what concordance is there between *general* and *particular*? Or with what sense can it be called "The Universal particular Church?" And yet they make their credulous followers believe that they cannot be of the Catholic Church unless they communicate with their particular Roman Church; clean contrary to the name and nature of the word "Catholic."

    The third consideration is that the Church is visible, and that in all ages: but it must be known how, and in what sense it may be truly said to be always visible; according to the Romish tenet, it is said to be visible, and palpable, as some eminent State, monarchy, or commonwealth, as Rome, France, or Venice, conspicuous in flourishing pomp to the eye of the world, so that it may at all times be sensibly discerned. But, alas, this conceit is a mere golden dream, and senseless dotage. For let an ingenuous mind, awakened once out of slumber, look seriously into the Word of God, and consider the state of the Church in all ages, he shall find for his satisfaction that the Church has oftentimes been obscured, captivated, persecuted, and so far from being acknowledged, that it has been accounted of the world no better than schism and heresy. And the true professors prosecuted as malefactors, for their soundness, as both the prophets, Christ himself, and the Apostles were, by the corrupt members of the visible Church, bearing the chief rule. To this effect the prophet Isaiah complained, that in his time the Church was but a small remnant. And those hooted at like owls, being as signs and wonders in Israel (Isa. 1:9; 8:18). The complaint of Elias is that he was left alone (Rom. 11:3). The faithful were glad to be hid in caves, and fed with bread and water by religious Obadiah (1 King 18:4, 13). And as it is in the Epistle to the Hebrews, "They wandered about in sheep skins, and goat skins, being destitute, afflicted, tormented, of whom the world was not worthy: they wandered in deserts, and in mountains, and in dens, and caves of the earth," (Heb. 11:37-38). The prophecies of the Christian Church foretell as much, both for outward persecutions, and open apostasy under one eminent head, called "That man of Sin," who should take on him to oppose and exalt himself above all that is called God, challenging the chief sovereignty in the Temple of the Church of God (2 Thess. 2:3-4). In St. John's vision, the Woman, the Church, was constrained through persecution to fly into the wilderness (Rev. 12: 6). Our Savior foreshows how hard it should be to find faith on the earth (Luke 18:8). How the faithful should be afflicted, killed, and hated of all nations: that iniquity shall abound and the love of many shall become cold. And that the cunning impostures of false teachers, pretending the name of Christ and the Church, should be such, and so specious, being seconded also with miracles, that if it were possible, the very elect should be deceived.

From this was the flourishing visibility of the Church, when the poison of Arianism had infected almost the whole world. Of which time, St. Jerome writes, "That the ship of the Church was almost sunk." And this some of our Romish adversaries confess, both at the time of Arian heresy, and in the time of Antichrist. Then, that we may not be seduced and carried away with flourishing shows, we must know that the Church, though it is always visible, yet it is not always alike visible. It is not always in pomp, and eminent estate. He that in the time of Christ should so have looked for the Church, would sooner have joined himself to the Jewish synagogue, than to the society of Christ and his Apostles. We must not therefore look so much to the multitude, and outward flourish, as seek for the truth, though it is but in a few, and though never so obscure. For it is not of necessity that the Church is always discerned and acknowledged of the world, but it is sufficient to the visibility of it, that it never fails to be visibly seen and acknowledged by the professors themselves: for this must ever hold in the Church, in the mildest of disturbances, that "wisdom is justified of her children," (Matt. 11:19).

The fourth consideration is that in the visible Church, some particular Churches are more pure, some more corrupt than others; as the Church of Corinth and Galatia, and some of the seven Asian Churches were more infected with error than other Churches. Under this head are to be observed diverse remarkable points, and very necessary for our present use.

1. That in a corrupt Church, sometimes the greatest member, and among them the most chief for eminence and authority are most corrupted. So it was in the idolatrous times among the Jews, "all the chief of the priests, and people, transgressed very much, after all the abominations of the heathen, and polluted the House of the Lord. They mocked the messengers of God, and despised his word, and misused his prophets," (2 Chron. 36:14, 16). It was so at the coming of Christ, "He came unto his own, and his own received him not," (John 1:11). No, they rejected him! "This," says St. Peter, "is the stone, which was set at naught of you builders," (Acts 4:11). The master builders were the chief destroyers: the prime governors in the Church, the greatest enemies of Christ, and

Christianity. So for a time the Arian faction prevailed against the true Church, having gotten the Imperial Throne to countenance them, by means whereof they did sway all things at their pleasure. And so it has been a long time, and continues to this day, in the Church of Rome. So that we may well say to them with Leo, "Ye are armed with the name of the Church," and yet "ye fight against the Church." This may advise us, that the truth of religion is not yet tied to multitude and greatness.

2. That where many excellent privileged and comfortable promises belong to the Church, we must know that the sound and good heart only, and not the corrupt, is capable of those benefits. "I dare not," St. Augustine says, speaking of the prerogatives of the Church, "understand this, but of just and holy men." Therefore, St. Paul ties privileges to the true Israel of God, the Children of Promise (Rom. 9:4, 6, 8). And St. Peter, the promises, to them that are effectually called (Acts 2:39). By this we may see, both that the chief and most eminent, yes and the greatest number in the Church, if they lack true saving grace, have no right to the privileges and promises of the Church, though they live in the midst of it. And again, the poorest member of the Church, that is a true believer, shall sustain no prejudice to hinder his happiness, by being mixed with the wicked. But the wheat shall be gathered into the Lord's garner, the chaff into the fire (Matt. 3:12). "For," says the Apostle, "what if some did not believe? Shall

their unbelief make the faith of God without effect?" (Rom. 3:3).

3. That a corrupt Church may keep, and convey to posterity the canon of Sacred Scripture, the form of knowledge, and the rule of faith, and wholesome doctrine and Sacraments in a general manner. And yet overthrow all by some particular opposite doctrines, and superstitious practices, to the loss of their own salvation, that so hold and practice. In the greatest depravation of religion by idolatry in the time of the Jews, it was so. The Book of God, though it lays dusty and out of use, yet by the providence of God it was kept. The sacraments, especially circumcision, was in use even in corrupt times, and hypocrites gloried in the outward circumcision, as we may see by the reproofs of the prophets and Apostles (Acts 15:21). The Jewish synagogue at the coming of our Lord kept these oracles, and that for us, though they did not think so (Rom. 3:2). "The Jew," St. Augustine says, "carrieth the Book, whereby the Christian may believe." Yes, they did teach many things in their subjects which were very sound, and therefore sitting in Moses's chair, by teaching Moses's doctrine, Christ would have them so far at least to be heard (Matt. 23:2-3). But yet for all this, mark what the Lord Jesus says of them, "Except your righteousness shall exceed the righteousness of the Scribes and Pharisees, ye shall in no case enter into the Kingdom of heaven," (Matt. 5:20). And

again, "In vain they worship me, teaching for doctrines, men's precepts," (Matthew 15:9).

On this it follows that by reason of these means, there may be in a corrupt Church, some that may preserve faith and true religion, for the substance, as did Zachariah the Priest, and Elizabeth his wife, old Simeon, Nathaniel, Joseph and Mary, and many more. And on this ground, we of the Reformed Churches think and judge charitably of our forefathers that lived in those blind and dark times of Popery, and of such as yet remain among them, or are entangled by them, on conceit of their common claim of the only Catholic Church: we, I say, judge charitably of them, though they detrude us all into Hell. For so we deem this their state before God: that as in the times of apostasy and falling into idolatry among the Jews, the Lord had a remnant. He reserved to himself seven thousand which never bowed the knee to Baal (Rom. 11:4). He had in the Church of Pergamos, even where Satan's throne was, those that kept his Name and did not deny his faith (Rev. 2:13): and that in the heat of persecution, he had a few names in Sardis, which had not defiled their garments (Rev. 3:4). So we do not doubt, but God ever had, has at this time, and shall have to the end, many, in the very midst of the Papacy, that do not know the whole mystery of Romish iniquity, but in simplicity of heart lay hold on Jesus Christ, and him alone, for their salvation. They see, according to that light they have, many corruptions and enormities, bewail them and shun them, as far as their strength and measure of knowledge and grace will permit. These, we say, holding the foundation, though they may build on it the hay or stubble of some errors and superstitions (not destroying the foundation) may be saved, though the mercy of God in Christ pardoning their sins of ignorance and error, on their general repentance. We may see the like in the Church of Thyatira, there were many that did not have that learning (as the false teachers in their vain-glorious bragging termed it) nor did know the deepness of Satan; but did hold fast to the main truth, though in much weakness: and all that God requires of them, is, that they are constant in it (Rev. 2:24-25). In the same manner the Lord speaks to the Church of Philadelphia, "Thou hast a little strength, and hast kept my Word, and hast not denied my Name," (Rev. 3:8). For God does not so much look to the measure and quantity of grace, as to the sincerity and soundness of it.

Many godly and learned among them did not by and by, on the sight of some corruptions, leave and forsake the society of the Church of Rome: Oecolampadius, Capito, Melancthon, and Luther himself; no, some of them continued in the outward communion of the Roman Church until their dying day, as Erasmus and others, who thought well of the cause or matter of Reformation, but did not approve separation being carried away with the main stream of the name of "Church," and "Mother Church." Do not marvel therefore, if among us, we have of meaner learning, or of the simpler sort, that so harp on that string, that they have no ear to hearken to Christ's pipe. It is no new thing, to see a child mistake, and cry out after a stranger instead of their own mother. So, why may it not be, that some in their simplicity may fall into such misprision, as to take the Romish Synagogue to be their Mother Church, being indeed not so much as a sound member of it, but as a disease, a pest or gangrene in the body?

It is apparent then, that in a corrupt Church some may be sound, and so be saved. And this we hold of the Church of Rome, as corrupt as it is: for our Lord would never have said of Spiritual Babylon, "Come out of her, my people," (Rev. 18:4), if he had none there. And let not our Romanists brag of this our ingenuous confession, and play on it, the better to seduce the simple. For in truth, it stands them in no more stead to patronize their impieties, then the Fathers approving of the Baptism of the Donatists and other heretics, countenanced their heresies. For what is the chaff the better, because it is acknowledged that there is some wheat hid among it? We do not say absolutely, there is salvation to be found in the Romish Babylon, but in the midst of so great confusion, there may be salvation for some. There is great difference between possibility of salvation, which may be in a corrupt Church, and infallibility, which is ever without doubt in the true and orthodox Church. Are any so simple as to commit his whole estate into a ship full of leaks, of which there is just cause of doubt, whether ever it shall safely arrive at the desired port; when he may transport it in a sound and safe vessel? Noah and all his, if they will not perish in the deluge, must get into the ark (Gen 7:13). Lot must not stay in Sodom, if he will be safe and free from the common judgment (Gen 19:15). The people of God must, for this very cause, come out of Spiritual Babylon, both for the danger of infection by sin; and destruction, by means of her plagues. Where therefore the doctrine is orthodox and sound, the religious worship, service, and Sacraments, for the truth and substance of them, the very same with the prime Churches, and best antiquity, as it is this day (blessed be God) in our Church of England, and the rest of the Reformed Churches, there is the surest and safest repose for the Christian soul: in this society there is infallible certainty of salvation. But in an apostatical and corrupt Church, as the Roman Church now is, it is not so, though yet God may reserve a remnant, pulling them, as it were, out of the fire; and that, with this caveat, that they do not tarry in Babylon (Jude 23).

So we have seen that salvation is only to be found in the Church; and what that Church is where salvation may be had.

HOW MEN MAY BE ADDED TO THE CHURCH

Now let us come to the third branch: that is, by what means, and how men are to be added to the Church, that they may be found.

The means are expressed in this context, and are these three: the Word preached, faith to apprehend it, and the Sacrament of Baptism to seal and confirm it (Acts 2:37-38, 41). This is all required for the admission of any into the Church: to hear, believe, and be baptized (Acts 18:8).

THE MINISTRY OF THE WORD

The ministry of the Word is the main ordinance of God, for the gathering together of the Saints, appointed of God to that end, and to continue in the Church to the end of the world (Eph. 4:13; Matt. 28:20). Therefore, it is called the incorruptible or immortal seed, by which we are regenerated and born again (1 Pet. 1:23); and "the Word of truth," (James 1:18), wherewith we are begotten of God, to become his dear children, and the first fruits of his creatures: Yes, it is, as St.

Paul calls it, "The power of God unto salvation," (Rom. 1:16). Therefore, when God would have any converted to the faith, he sends them to this means. Philip is commanded to join himself near to the chariot of the eunuch, that by his preaching the eunuch might be joined to Christ and his Church. St. Peter is sent for to Cornelius, to teach him and his the way to heaven by Christ. St. Paul must tarry at Corinth, to teach the Word of God among them, "For," says the Lord, "I have much people in this city," (Acts 18:10). And indeed, the converting of souls is a great work; and great works had need of potent and mighty means: therefore it pleases God to use his powerful Word, which, as the Apostle says, is mighty through God, to the pulling down of strongholds, and casting down of imaginations, and every high thing that exalts itself against the knowledge of God, and bringing into captivity every thought to the obedience of Christ (2 Cor. 10:4-5).

This calls the *teacher* to a serious consideration of the weight of his calling, and a conscionable regard to discharge it; he is put in trust with the precious souls of men, for whom he must give an account unto God. He is made God's steward, and therefore must be faithful (Heb. 13:17). He must not keep away the Bread of Life from God's family (1 Cor. 4:1-2). The word of reconciliation is committed to him (2 Cor. 5:19): yes necessity is laid on him, so that, though he is as great at St.

Paul himself, yet woe be unto him, if he "preach not the Gospel," (1 Cor. 9:16).

This consideration, that the Ministry of the Word is the means of our life. O what esteem should it cause that sacred calling to be of among men! How beautiful should their feet be, that bring glad tidings of peace! How amiable their presence, that present us to God in Christ (Col 1: 28)! What have we, or can we give to them, proportionable to the good we receive from God by them, being instrumentally the very saviors of our souls (1 Tim. 4:16)? Who can open the mouth, or lift up the hand despitefully against such, to whom hell itself is constrained to give this applause, "These men are the servants of the most high God, which show unto us the way of salvation," (Acts 16:16)?

The neglect of hearing the Word, no contempt, must therefore necessarily be a heinous sin, whatever salve or excuse may be laid on it. "For if the word spoken by angels was steadfast, and every transgression and disobedience received a just recompense of reward: how shall we escape, if we neglect so great a salvation," offered to us in the Ministry of the Gospel of Christ (Heb. 2:2-3)? Such men as so reject, and push the Word of God away from them, if we will believe the Apostle, pronounce a dire sentence against themselves; for by the very act of neglect, and contempt of the Word, "they judge themselves unworthy of everlasting life," (Act 13:46).

Then how careful ought we to be, to attend on the ordinance of God in the ministry of the Word? Let the preaching of the cross be to the profane world, to them that perish, "foolishness" but, the Apostle says, "unto us that are saved, it is the power of God," (1 Cor. 1:18). For so it has pleased God, by that which vain men set so light by, even by the "foolishness of preaching, to save them that believe." Let every soul, therefore, that would be partaker of the grace of life, neglect no good opportunity of hearing. Consider that eternal life consists in the knowledge of God in Christ, and as all learning, so heavenly knowledge must enter into the heart by care, the sense of hearing being the organ or instrument of learning (John 17:3). Set down then this resolution in your heart, with the faithful in the Psalm; "I will hear what God the Lord shall speak: for he will speak peace unto his people, and to his Saints: but let not them turn again to folly," (Psa. 85:8).

BELIEVING THE WORD

The second means of entrance into the Church is by believing. This must follow hearing, and go before baptism; for without faith, neither is the Word of force to us, nor we fit for Baptism. "The Word preached," the Apostle says, "did not profit them, not being mixed with faith in them that heard it,"

(Heb. 4:2). And the eunuch desiring baptism, is told by Philip, that he must first be a believer, "If thou believest," he says, "with all thy heart, thou mayest," (Acts 8:37). Look into the examples of all that ever were added to the Church, if they will be sound members, they must believe, no, they cannot so much as be admitted into the outward society, but they must at least profess faith, yes even Simon Magus himself. So "Crispus believed on the Lord, with all his house. Many of the Corinthians hearing, believed, and were baptized," (Acts 18:13); and so all of the rest of the converts to Christianity. And there is great reason for it; for no man can be added to the body of the Church, to become a sound member of it, but he must be united to the Head Christ Jesus, in whom all the members grown up into a complete body (Eph. 4:15-16). Now we are united unto Christ by none other means, but by faith, whereby he dwells in our hearts (Eph. 3:17).

Again, what is the Church, but a company of believers, a congregation of faithful men? Therefore, unless a man believe, he cannot be of that society. Besides, the Word is the bread of life, the food of the soul; so that as natural food cannot sustain nature, unless it is received into the body and digested; no more can the Word be a Word of life to the soul, expect it is apprehended by faith. It is a saving Word only to them that believe (1 Cor. 1:21).

They therefore, that hearing, do not believe, are in the same or rather worse condition, than they that do not hear at all. For sins of knowledge are greater than sins of ignorance, and the means, not profited by, aggravates the sin. Yet the sentence is fearful. That "He that believeth not, shall be damned," (Mark 16:16). And the very same Word that is by unbelief so rejected, shall judge the incredulous (they that receive it not by faith) at the last day (John 12:48).

This should movingly persuade every Christian soul to mix the Word with faith: considering that, as the means of uniting to the Church, on God's part, is the lively voice of his Word preached, so on man's part the effectual means is faith. No, God for our greater encouragement has promised to his, both the means, and the efficacy of it. For the means, see the prophet Isaiah, "Though," says the prophet, "the Lord give you the bread of adversity, and the water of affliction, yet shall not thy teachers be moved into a corner anymore, but thine eyes shall see thy teachers: and thine ears shall hear a word behind thee, saying, 'This is the way, walk in it'," (Isa. 30:20-21). And as for the efficacy, God has bound himself so to assist his outward ordinance, that his inward working grace shall concur with it, "I will put my Law in their inward parts, and write it in their hearts," says the Lord (Jer. 31:33).

This also may be a touchstone, to try us, whether we are indeed united to the Church of God, or in outward show only. For we see evidently, that none are incorporated into the body of Christ, but the true believers. And who are those true believers? Take these brief notes of them.

1. A true believer relies only on the mercy of God in Christ, whose mercy he so accounts his all-sufficient merit, that he professes unfeignedly, that he has none in heaven but the Lord, and none on earth but he (Psa. 73:25).
2. The true believer lives no longer in the former course of his ignorance and sin, he does not walk after the flesh, but after the Spirit, becoming, by the power of the death of Christ, dead to sin.
3. The true believer expresses his faith by his works: knowing that it is not idle, but works by love.
4. The true believer is constant in his way of piety and virtue, that he may attain to the end of his faith, the salvation of his soul: for he well knows, that he cannot receive the crown of life, unless he is faithful to death.

BAPTISM

The sacrament of baptism is the third means of entering into the Church; for the *covenant* being propounded in the Word, and accepted and embraced of the believer by faith, is ratified and confirmed by the seal of baptism; and so salvation, as by a deed under hand and seal, is effectually conveyed unto us. Therefore, baptism is called by St. Peter, "the like figure, which now saveth us," (1 Pet. 3:21), because it is not a naked or bare sign of our regeneration and salvation, but an effectual seal, organ, and instrument, to convey, and as it were, to set the very stamp and character of saving grace on the soul of every faithful Christian. It is here said of St. Ambrose, "The original of true life, and of true righteousness, is grounded on the Sacrament of Regeneration." Suitable to this antiquity, is the modern doctrine of our Christian Church. Baptism (says our Church of England) is not only a sign of "profession, and mark of difference...but is also a sign of regeneration or new birth, whereby, as by an instrument, they that receive Baptism rightly, are grafted into the Church, *etc.*," (Article 27). Yes, Calvin himself is so plain, for the efficacy of the Sacrament, and to show that it is not a bare sign; that he proves out of the Epistle to the Romans, that by Christian Baptism Christ has made us partakers of his death, that we may be grafted into it. And immediately after, in the very next words he says they that receive Baptism with such faith as they ought, do truly feel the efficacy of Christ's death, even as the young graft receives sap from the stock into which it is set. And afterward he calls baptism, with St. Paul, the laver or washing of regeneration and renovation (Titus 3:5): noting by it the force of baptism.

Again, Calvin in another place, defending the baptism of infants against Anabaptists, and speaking of the state of infants in baptism, says that Christ, to the end may make infants capable of life. He makes them partakers of himself. And a little after he takes away this Anabaptistic objection. How can infants be regenerate, say the Anabaptists, seeing they know neither good nor evil? Where Calvin answers, the work of God, though it is not subject to our capacity, yet it does not therefore cease to be.

So we see that baptism is an effectual means of our entrance into the Church of God. They are therefore worthy of severe reproof who, either out of error, undervaluing the excellency of this sacrament, or through negligence, conceiting there is no such necessity of it, do sinfully omit and defer the seasonable use of baptism. Such must suffer themselves to be informed in the truth, and know, that there is as express a mandate for Baptism, as there is for teaching, hearing, praying, or any other pious or moral duty. He that said, "Go and teach," said also, "Baptize them," (Matt. 28:19-20). The Apostle did not simply say to those whom he directed in the way to salvation, "Repent ye," but with it he adds, and "be baptized every one of you, for the remission of sins," (Acts 2:38). And it was according to the Lord's charge given in the Apostle's commission: which is, that they teach me to observe whatsoever he had commanded them. So then, though it is not of that absolute necessity, that infants dying without it, when it cannot conveniently be had, should be damned, according to the Romish bloody position: yet seeing there is the necessity of precept, men must take heed of neglecting so weighty a duty. If the Jew, for the neglect of Circumcision was to be cut off, how shall the Christian be excusable (Gen 17:14)? How shall he escape for the omitting of so great a Sacrament (Heb. 2:3)?

THE AUTHOR OF THIS ADDITION TO THE CHURCH

So we have seen the means by which men are added to the Church, the Word, faith, and Baptism. The next point is, The Author of this addition; and that is, the Lord: the Lord added to the Church such as should be saved. The Rhemists add the pronoun, *our* Lord, as their usual manner is, contrary to the vulgar Latin edition, which yet they pretend in their translation exactly to follow. It is in truth a gross abuse of the sacred Text to add so many hundred pronouns, more than ever God made; and yet cavil at our translation for turning it into the word "congregation," where it is the most proper signification of the word. But it is worth the noting, to observe how they are constrained sometimes to translate "the Lord," and not "our Lord," seeing in themselves the absurdity of it: as in Matthew, where it is said, "The Lord said unto my Lord," (Matt. 22:44); there they leave out the pronoun, perceiving how odd and harsh the tone would be, to translate it, "Our Lord said to my Lord." These pronounists so glory in the phrase, that it becomes a distinguishing note of a Romish Catholic, insomuch that if any will sympathize with them, he must speak in their language, as some do, to please them.

To come to the point, it is the Lord that adds to the Church such as shall be saved. God must persuade Japheth. It is he that must enlarge him, that he may dwell in the tents of Shem (Gen 9:27). He gives to Christ such as are ordained to life (John 17:6); otherwise there is a plain impossibility of our union with Christ and his Church. For our Savior peremptorily affirms that no man can come to him, except the Father draws him; and except it is given to him of his Father (John 6:44, 65). The means without this *efficient* cannot be effectual. "Paul planted, Apollos watered, but God gave the increase;" without whom, neither he that plants is anything, neither he that waters (1 Cor. 3:6-7). God opened the heart of Lydia, before she could profitably attend to St. Paul's preaching (Acts 16:14). If his Spirit does not inwardly work together with the outward voice, it shall but beat the air in vain.

The reason is evident: for man's deadness is such, that he can no more move toward heaven, so much as one step, than a dead man can rise of himself (Eph. 2:1-2)

No, there is in the corrupt nature of man, an opposite disposition and willingness to remain in the state of sin, like Lot to linger in Sodom: so that there is naturally a reluctation and striving against the work of grace: which remaining in the regenerate in part, causes them, that they cannot always do the good that they would.

Again, the work of conversion and regeneration is a miraculous work, greater than the work of creation, and therefore requires a divine power to effect it. In the first creation there was no life: God said the word, and the creatures had their being instantly: but in the work of regeneration, there are many obstacles such as Satan, the world, the flesh—not that anything can hinder the effect of God's omnipotence, but in respect of us.

This confutes the error of freedom of the will to do good in man by nature; whether wholly, as the Pelagians held; or in part, as our Romanists maintain. The right Christian and catholic verity is, with St. Paul, by a negative, to exclude nature, and extoll grace, by which nature of nilling, is made willing (1 Cor. 15:10). "For it is God that works in us both do will and to do," (Phil 2:13). "We will," says an early Father, "but God doth give us that power to will."

Is any man partaker of this grace, is he drawn of God, has the Lord added him to his Church? Let him give his Name the praise, and confess with the Apostle, that he has obtained mercy (1 Tim. 1:13). For indeed it is a great mercy of God, to be taken out of the slavery and bondage of Satan, and to be put into the Lord's service, which is perfect freedom, and has for the end, everlasting life (Rom. 6:12).

BE UNITED TO CHRIST

To conclude this point; does any desire to be sincerely united to the Church of Christ? Let him go to the fountain of this grace, and cry with them in the Song of Solomon, "Draw me, we will run after thee," (Song 1:4). And with David, "Unite my heart, to fear thy name," (Psa. 86:11). And with the prodigal, "O Lord, make me as one of thy household servants."

The time of this addition to the Church is here said to be daily, or from day to day: it shall not fail, to the last day, nor time be anymore, when the number of the elect is once complete (Matt. 24:22). Yet it is not so to be understood, as if the increase of the Church should be always apparent, and in a flourishing eminency, as our Rhemists on this text would have it. For we know by the Word of God, that there must be apostasy and falling into error, in these last times, as was said before.

The consideration of the time is of excellent use. It shows the patience of God, in waiting so long from day to day for conversion (2 Pet. 3:9). It was great to the old world, when the long-suffering of God waited in the days of Noah, by the space of 120 years (1 Pet. 3:20; Gen 6:5); but it was nothing to the time of the Gospel, from the first, to the second coming of Christ. This advises us to take special notice of the day of our visitation. "For through the tender mercy of our God, the dayspring from on high hath visited us," (Luke 1:78). Do we have the light? Let us walk in it, while we have it, and pray the Lord to send it, to them that sit in darkness.

Again, let us not rashly censure, nor uncomfortably despair of those that are without: the Lord adds to his Church daily. Therefore let us, while there is time, both hope, and help forward the work of God. All are not called in the prime of the day, but some at the third, some at the sixth, some at the eleventh hour (Matt. 20:3-6). He that is today, with Saul, a persecutor, may be tomorrow a convert, and profess that which before he persecuted. We say, "He runs far, that never returns," but know, that none can outrun God, when he will fetch him home to himself.

To close up this matter in brief; see here in the last place, the happiness of those that are added to the Church: it is in one word, "salvation;" being made the servants of God, and becoming of his family, which is the Church, They have says the Apostle, their "fruit in holiness, and the end, everlasting life," (Rom. 6:22). They are kept by the power of God, through faith, unto salvation. They are safe in the Ark, while the world of the wicked perish in the Deluge. They are in the little Zoar of God's Church, out of the danger of the fire of God's wrath (Gen 19:22). Happy are the people that are in such a case, yea thrice happy are they that have the Lord for their God (Psa. 144:15).

What can allure us to be of this society, if this motive of eternal happiness does not prevail with us? Men desire to be free of those corporations that have great immunities ad privileges: then know, that no city can compare with the heavenly Jerusalem: no society can compare to the Communion of Saints.

How profane, then, and blasphemous is the conceit of wicked worldlings, that say, "it is vain to serve God: and what profit is in religion and religious walking before the Lord?" and count the proud and wicked, like themselves, the only happy men? (Mal. 3:14; Job 21:14). What a lamentable thing it is, that the *god* of the world should so blind their eyes, that they should not see their own misery, and the contrary happiness of God's people, until with the rich glutton, it is too late (2 Cor. 1:4; Luke 16:23)!

As for those that have their part in this happiness, let them go on cheerfully, "abounding in the work of the Lord: forasmuch as they know, that their labor is not in vain in the Lord," (1 Cor. 15:58). Let them from the bottom of their hearts say, "Blessed be the God and Father of our Lord Jesus Christ, which according to his abundant mercy, hath begotten us again unto a lively hope, by the resurrection of Jesus Christ from the dead, to an inheritance incorruptible and undefiled, and that fadeth not away, reserved in heaven for us," (1 Pet. 1:3-4). Amen.

www.ingramcontent.com/pod-product-compliance
Lightning Source LLC
Chambersburg PA
CBHW032005080426
42735CB00007B/514